DECLARATIONS OF TRUST:
A DRAFTSMAN'S HANDBOOK

AUSTRALIA
Law Book Co. — Sydney

CANADA and **USA**
Carswell — Toronto

HONG KONG
Sweet & Maxwell Asia

NEW ZEALAND
Brookers — Wellington

SINGAPORE and **MALAYSIA**
Sweet & Maxwell Asia
Singapore and Kuala Lumpur

DECLARATIONS OF TRUST:
A DRAFTSMAN'S HANDBOOK

Edited by Catherine Sanders

THOMSON
TM
SWEET & MAXWELL

First edition William M. Hartley 1995
Second edition edited by Catherine Sanders 2001
Third edition edited by Catherine Sanders 2005

Published in 2005 by
Sweet & Maxwell Limited
100 Avenue Road, Swiss Cottage,
London NW3 3PF

Typeset by LBJ Typesetting Ltd. of Kingsclere
Printed and bound in Great Britain
by TJ International, Padstow, Cornwall

No natural forests were destroyed to make this product, only farmed timber was used and re-planted.

ISBN 0 421 88990 X

A CIP catalogue record for this book is available from The British Library.

Contents

Contents   ix

x   Contents

Preface

Many years ago, as a fairly new qualified solicitor in private practice, I advised the parties to a property purchase to clarify their interests by means of a declaration of trust. However, when I came to draft the document for them, I was surprised to discover that no precedent was to be found and that I would have to start from scratch. I therefore breathed a sigh of relief when William Hartley produced the excellent first edition of this book in 1995. I read it immediately from cover to cover and have referred to it many times during my career.

I am delighted to have been asked to produce a third edition to reflect changes in the law, principally those brought about by the Land Registration Act 2002 and Land Registration Rules 2003, but also the new Stamp Duty regime, including Stamp Duty Land Tax. The chapter on secret trusts has also been expanded to include some material on mutual wills. For the first time the precedents are available on an accompanying CD-ROM.

My thanks go the author for embarking on the difficult task of producing the original text and to Sweet and Maxwell for again inviting me to update it. I hope that the book and CD-ROM continue to be of practical help to overworked solicitors, particularly those general and conveyancing practitioners who may not have ready access to trust expertise or simply do not want to bother their colleagues.

The views expressed in this edition are in a personal and not an official capacity.

The law is as stated at July 1, 2005.

Catherine Sanders,
London, July 2005

Table of Cases

References are to paragraph numbers

TABLE OF CASES

Table of Statutes

References are to paragraph numbers

Table of Statutory Instruments

References are to paragraph numbers

1

General principles

1. Introduction

Declarations of trust are most commonly used to set out the interests of parties where an asset is held by more than one person. The parties may decide that the benefit of the assets should be held in equal shares or in some other proportion. Thus, a declaration of trust can be used when a couple set up home together or when there is a joint venture. Similarly an asset may have been purchased jointly and the parties may decide that their interests should be more specifically defined so that the property does not pass to the survivor of them on death. A declaration of trust has further value in that equitable ownership in an asset may pass to another while legal title remains where it is.

The making of a declaration of trust can often be viewed as the tidying up of the file; the main transaction is completed and the parties appear clear about what is intended when the period of the trust comes to an end. All too often the making of the declaration is put on one side. Its importance can be overlooked until there is either disagreement between the parties or with third parties, such as the Inland Revenue or a trustee in bankruptcy. It is only then that the value of the declaration comes into its own, for not only may it regulate the interests in the asset between the parties concerned but it provides evidence of entitlement.

The aim of this book is to provide some precedents so that the tidying up process is made easier and is actually done, and also to provide indications as to the uses of declarations of trust. Inevitably the precedents that follow only touch on the most common situations. Before turning to the separate chapters and precedents, it might be helpful to refer to various general points, some of which can help to emphasise the role of a declaration of trust.

1–001

1–002

1–003

In these days of equality, it is important to emphasise that the masculine includes the feminine and vice versa (Interpretation Act 1978, s.6); similarly, no discrimination is intended and the precedents should be capable of adaptation, whatever the relationship of the parties.

2. THE CERTAINTIES OF A TRUST

1–004 The declarations of trust contained in this book each constitute an express trust, many of them for the persons actually making the declaration. It is important to remember the three certainties necessary to constitute an express trust:

(1) certainty of words *i.e.*, the declaration must indicate that a trust is intended;

(2) certainty of the subject matter of the trust (see *Hunter v Moss* [1994] 1 W.L.R. 452; below p.124); and

(3) certainty of beneficiaries.

Whilst trusts of pure personalty may be constituted by oral declarations, any declaration of trust respecting land or any interest therein must be in writing signed by some person who is able to declare such trusts (Law of Property Act 1925, s.53).

However, a written declaration gives a greater chance of certainty for assets which are not land, not least because the parties have to consider what is to be contained in the declaration.

3. RESULTING TRUSTS AND PRESUMPTION OF ADVANCEMENT

1–005 An implied or resulting trust arises where, on a purchase, property is conveyed into the name of someone other than the person who provides the purchase money. The result of this is that a trust of the legal estate results to the person who provides the purchase money. Contribution to the purchase price at the date of acquisition is the vital consideration and mortgage repayments made by a joint owner at a later date will not rebut a resulting trust arising in favour of a sole contributor. (*Carlton v Goodman* [2002]EWCA Civ. 545) However from December 5, 2005, under the Civil Partnerships Act 2004, where a civil partner makes a substantial financial contribution to the improvement of a property owned by either or both partner, he will be treated as having acquired a share unless there is an express or implied agreement to the contrary.

The doctrine applies to personalty as well as land (*Re Scottish Equitable Life Assurance Society* [1902] 1 Ch.282). It also applies where two or more persons provide purchase money jointly and the purchase is taken in the name of one only, with the resulting trust arising in favour of the persons who provided the money. The case of *Lohia v Lohia* [2001] W.T.L.R. 101 confirmed that in the case of land only the presumption will not arise where the conveyance is voluntary and not on purchase. The doctrine of resulting trusts will not apply where the relationship existing between the person who provided the purchase money and the person in whose name the asset was purchased is such as to raise a presumption that a gift was intended.

The presumption of advancement arises if a husband purchases a **1–006** property in the name of a wife, or a father purchases a property in the name of a child. In the absence of evidence to the contrary, the presumption of advancement would presume that a gift was intended to be made. The concept of advancement which applies to only very limited relationships seems wholly outdated and its application to modern situations can lead to some arbitrary results (see *Tinsley v Milligan* [1994] A.C. 340).

Both the presumptions of resulting trust and of advancement can be rebutted by evidence of the purchaser's actual intention at purchase as to beneficial ownership. However, the presumptions are still significant and offer a clear reason why declarations of trust should be made.

4. INSOLVENCY

A transaction effected at an undervalue (for example a gift) can **1–007** be set aside, on the application of a trustee in bankruptcy, if it took place within two years prior to the presentation of the bankruptcy petition; if it took place within five years prior to the presentation of the petition and the individual was insolvent at the time of the transaction; or became insolvent because of it or whenever it took place if it was made with the intention of putting assets beyond the reach of creditors. The court has a discretion as to the appropriate order to make and is not necessarily required to set the transaction aside completely (Insolvency Act 1986, ss.339–342, ss.423–4).

5. MATRIMONIAL AND INHERITANCE ACT PROCEEDINGS

1–008 Declarations of trust made other than for valuable consideration with the intention of defeating a spouse's claim for financial relief in matrimonial proceedings (or from December 5, 2005 that of a civil partner) are also vulnerable to being set aside (Matrimonial Causes Act 1973, s.37). Similarly, a declaration containing an element of gift intended to defeat claims under the Inheritance (Provision for Family and Dependants) Act 1975 may be set aside if made within six years of the settlor's death (see Inheritance (Provision for Family and Dependants) Act 1975, s.10 and the recent unreported case of *Afsar v Khan*, June 2, 1999).

6. LEGAL TITLE

1–009 Legal title to land can only be held by four persons (Law of Property Act 1925, s.34(2)) as amended by Trusts of Land and Appointment of Trustees Act 1996, s.5(1), Sch.2, para.3(1),(2). Where more than four people are to have an interest in land, then the interests of all should be set out in a separate document, such as a declaration of trust or partnership agreement.

It is not unusual for a party to borrow money to buy his share. The lender will naturally want security by taking a charge on the underlying property (and thus from the four legal owners), and they in turn will require an indemnity from the borrowing party which can be dealt with in the declaration of trust setting out the various parties' interests.

7. TRUSTS OF LAND

Until the Trusts of Land and Appointment of Trustees Act 1996 came into force on January 1, 1997, land held by two or more persons was held upon a statutory trust for sale under ss.34–36 of the Law of Property Act 1925. From that date, land conveyed to co-owners either as beneficial joint tenants or tenants in common is held on a trust of land (Trusts of Land and Appointment of

Trustees Act 1996, ss.1 and 5). The co-owners have the powers of an absolute owner in relation to the property (Trusts of Land and Appointment of Trustees Act 1996, s.6 as amended by the Trustee Act 2000) which include a more evenly balanced power of sale and power of retention. Although it is possible to create express trusts for sale it is not possible to exclude the power to postpone sale.

8. Tax

Whilst this book does not set out to be a tax book, tax should **1–010** never be far from the practitioner's mind when advising his client. With regard to tax, the following points should be borne in mind. In addition, it should be noted that from December 5, 2005 civil partners under the Civil Partnership Act 2004 will be treated the same as married couples for tax purposes.

(a) Income Tax

The declaration of trust can be particularly relevant in arranging affairs judiciously for income tax purposes where property which produces income is held by husband and wife (see further Ch.2). In non husband and wife situations care should be taken to ensure that an income tax charge under the pre-owned assets regime does not apply (see further, Reservation of Benefit below).

(b) Capital Gains Tax

A declaration of trust which in effect disposes of a party's interest in an asset (whether in whole or in part) is a disposal for Capital Gains Tax purposes. It is appropriate therefore to be aware of the exemptions and reliefs.

(i) Spouses living together

There is no charge to Capital Gains Tax on a transfer of assets **1–011** between husband and wife provided that they are living together in the year of assessment in which the transfer takes place (Taxation of Chargeable Gains Act 1992, s.58). Thus, where property is held by one party to the marriage and subsequently declared to be held for both parties, no charge to Capital Gains Tax would arise on that effective transfer.

(ii) Only or main residence

Gains accruing on the disposal of, or an interest in, a dwelling-house which is or has been an individual's only or main residence (together with gardens or grounds of up to half a hectare in extent or other extent required for the reasonable enjoyment of the residence according to the size and character of the dwelling-house) throughout the period of ownership are exempt from Capital Gains Tax (Taxation of Chargeable Gains Act 1992, s.222). The last 36 months of ownership are disregarded for this purpose. Thus, a disposal through the medium of a declaration of trust (see Ch.4) in such a case would not incur a liability to Capital Gains Tax.

(iii) Annual exemption

1–012 There is an annual exemption of £8500 in 2005/6 available for each party holding an interest in a property. It is helpful to be able to prove to the Inland Revenue the extent of that interest by way of a declaration of trust.

(iv) Hold over relief

In the case of company shares remaining in the name of the registered shareholder but held for another (see Ch.6), it should be considered whether or not hold over relief for Capital Gains Tax purposes may be available on the transfer of the interest which occurs on the making of the declaration (Taxation of Chargeable Gains Act 1992, s.165).

Hold over relief is available where there is a disposal by an individual either by way of gift or by way of a sale at undervalue, and the relief is limited to gifts of business assets (Taxation of Chargeable Gains Act 1992, s.165(2)). Non-business assets do not attract relief and that part of the gain on a disposal of shares in a company which owns non business assets is therefore excluded from relief, a point often overlooked.

A claim for hold over relief under the section will have to be made by both transferor and transferee.

(v) Taper Relief

Capital gains may be reduced by taper relief, the reduction increasing the longer the asset has been held after April 5, 1998.

More generous taper relief is given for business assets. Indexation allowance is also available where assets were held prior to April 5, 1998.

(c) Inheritance Tax

A chargeable transfer for Inheritance Tax purposes can occur on **1–013** the making of a declaration of trust whereby the transferor's estate is reduced, so that it is appropriate to be aware of the exemptions and reliefs.

(i) Potentially exempt transfer

An absolute gift to a donee is a potentially exempt transfer for **1–014** Inheritance Tax purposes (Inheritance Tax Act 1984, s.3A(1)) and would generally therefore fall out of charge for IHT purposes if the donor survives the gift by seven years. If death occurs within the seven-year period the recipient is primarily liable for any tax referable to the gift (s.199(1)(b)). As the tax can be collected from the donor's personal representatives, it is not unusual for the donor to require an indemnity from the donee to pay any such tax.

(ii) Husband and wife

If both husband and wife are domiciled in the United Kingdom, any transfer of assets between them is exempt from any charge to Inheritance Tax (IHTA 1984, s.18(1)).

(iii) Nil-rate band

The first £275,000 of a person's estate is taxed at a nil rate for 2005/6, and the nil rate band is set to rise to £285,000 in 2006/07 and £300,000 in 2007/8. It is appropriate that where a husband and wife hold a house which has valuable equity then, if held as beneficial joint tenants, the tenancy should be severed so as to ensure at the very least that in the event of common accident their respective interests go under their respective wills (thus hopefully taking advantage of the nil band in each case). Therefore, to prove the extent of their interest, there should be a declaration of trust following the severance. In a non husband and wife situation where a sole owner makes a declaration of trust in favour of another then the provisions mentioned above should be considered. The main point however is that any declaration of trust is evidential as to the extent of the interests of the beneficiary concerned.

(iv) Reservation of benefit

Reservation of benefit rules were introduced by s.102 of the Finance Act 1986 and may apply to gifts made by declaration of trust. Where after March 17, 1986 an individual disposes of any property and either:

(1) possession and enjoyment of the property is not bona fide assumed by the donee at least seven years before the donor's death or on the date of the gift if later; or

(2) at any time within seven years of the donor's death, or if later, after the gift is made, the property is not enjoyed to the entire exclusion or virtually to the entire exclusion of the donor and of any benefit to him by contract or otherwise,

then the property will be treated as part of the individual's estate on his death.

In the case of property which is an interest in land or a chattel, retention or actual possession is disregarded for the purposes of para.(2), above if it is for full consideration in money or money's worth (Finance Act 1986, Sch.20, para.6(1)(a)). The rules in relation to land were extended following the House of Lords decision in *Ingram v IRC* [2000] 1 A.C. 293 for gifts made after March 8, 1999 (Finance Act 1986, ss.102A and B) and it should be noted that a gift of an undivided share in land is treated as a gift with reservation where the donor occupies without giving full consideration unless he occupies jointly with the donee and receives no material benefit (such as the payment of outgoings) at the donor's expense. Yet more anti-avoidance provisions were introduced by Finance Act 2003, (see Finance Act 1986,s.105A–C) following the Court of Appeal's decision in *IRC v Eversden* [2003] E.W.C.A. Civ 668.

(v) Pre-owned assets

Where property subject to a declaration of trust escapes the reservation of benefit provisions it may be caught by the pre-owned assets regime introduced by Finance Act 2004, Sch.15. From April 5, 2005, where an individual is in occupation of land or possession of chattels and either previously owned such asset or contributed to its purchase by another person, an annual charge to income tax can arise based on its rental value. It is possible, and may be beneficial in some cases, to opt out of the pre-owned assets regime and into the Inheritance Tax reservation of benefit provisions which must be done on or before to January 31, 2007. For a further consideration of the application of the rules to declarations of trusts of chattels see Ch.7.

(d) Stamp Duty and Stamp Duty Land Tax

Prior to Finance Act 2003, in general, declarations of trust **1–015** attracted fixed duty of £5 (Finance Act 1999, Sch.13, para.17). From December 1, 2003, Stamp Duty only applies to instruments relating to stock or marketable securities (Finance Act 2003, s.125) and therefore only declarations of trust relating to shares will continue to be liable to the £5 charge. *Ad valorem* duty is also still payable on declarations of trusts of shares characterised as sales for stamp duty purposes.

The Finance Act 2003 also introduced Stamp Duty Land Tax (SDLT) which is payable on land transactions other than those which are exempt under Sch.3 of the Act and require a self certificate on form SDLT 60. However, a declaration of trust relating to land which does not itself a effect a transfer will not be chargeable to SDLT or require a certificate, and in some cases utilising a declaration of trust may avoid the SDLT that would otherwise be payable on a transfer of the legal title (see further at p.82).

9. PARTIES TO THE DECLARATION

Where an individual declares that he holds an asset (or an interest in it) for another, the question may be raised as to whether or not the recipient needs to be a party to the declaration. Obviously the recipient must be a party where, for instance, he is giving an indemnity to the declarer.

It is thought to be prudent for the recipient to be a party in all cases, as not only does this confirm acceptance of the gift (if it is a gift situation), but it confirms agreement of the interests to be taken in the property which is the subject of the declaration.

10. REGISTERED AND UNREGISTERED LAND

1–016   All of England and Wales is now subject to compulsory registration of title. The types of transaction requiring registration were
greatly extended by the Land Registration Act 1997, and further
by the Land Registration Act 2002, s.4. As conveyances for
valuable or other consideration, by way of gift or pursuant to a
Court Order, are subject to first registration there will be very few
instances where a declaration of trust of newly acquired property
will concern unregistered land. In addition, the definition of "gift"
now specifically includes a transfer to trustees on trusts other than
bare trusts (see Land Registration Act 2002, s.4(7)). However, a
large number of unregistered titles remain and there will still be
situations where parties wish to define their interests in unregistered land by way of declaration of trust. Both types of land
have therefore been considered in all of the precedents for
consistency except where otherwise stated.

2

Property purchased as tenants in common

1. INTRODUCTION

There are many reasons why real property purchased jointly **2–001** should be held by the purchasers as tenants in common and why the respective shares should be defined by a declaration of trust.

(a) Interest of a person entitled to a share of sale proceeds

A declaration of trust should make it clear as to the respective interests of the co-owners so that in the event of a split of co-habitees or partners, the division of the proceeds of sale is beyond dispute. It will be appreciated that very often a property is purchased in the names of two persons and whilst they may hold it for themselves as tenants in common (for instance cohabitees or two sisters), they may hold it for several people (for instance six partners in a doctor's practice).

Where the property is a matrimonial asset or owned by civil partners other factors come into play, although the declaration may be useful evidence as to who provided the purchase monies in the first place.

(b) Devolution on death

The share of a deceased co-owner will devolve in accordance with **2–002** his will or on intestacy or in accordance with the terms of the declaration of trust.

(c) Inheritance Tax

The declaration of trust provides evidence as to the shares of the owners of the property.

(d) Insolvency

In the event of the insolvency of one of the owners, the declaration provides evidence as to what percentage of the proceeds of sale belong to the bankrupt's estate.

(e) Income Tax

2–003   It is useful to define the shares so that any rental income can be returned accordingly. It is generally assumed by the Inland Revenue that income from property held jointly by husband and wife, or from December 5, 2005, civil partners under the Civil Partnership Act (other than shares in a close company, see Ch.6) should be split 50/50 (Income and Corporation Taxes Act 1988, s.282A). A declaration of trust provides evidence to the contrary, although notification must be given to the Revenue within 60 days on Inland Revenue Form 17 (ICTA 1988, s.282B(3)). Conversely, if no notification is given, then even if the shares are not equal, husband and wife are taxed on the 50/50 basis which could be useful in providing the wife with an income for tax purposes (at lower rate) even though the asset is owned (say) 75 per cent by the husband.

For non husband and wife, the declaration provides the appropriate evidence for a split of the income.

(f) Capital Gains Tax

The declaration of trust evidences the ownership of the respective interests for capital gains tax purposes.

2. The Legal Title

2–004   It has been mentioned that the shares of joint holders of property should be defined by a declaration of trust (see above). The whole purpose of the original 1925 property legislation was to keep equitable interests off the legal title and indeed the Land Registration Act 2002 s.78 replicates the 1925 Act to provide that so far as possible, references to trusts shall be excluded from the Register.

(a) Unregistered land

2–005   The conveyance to the parties who hold the property would normally have declared that they were to hold the same "as tenants in common in equal shares" (or as the case may be), or alternatively that it was to be held by them as trustees "upon the trusts of a declaration of trust of even date to be executed immediately after this Deed".

In practice it is often some time before a declaration is executed—the priority has been to complete the conveyance. In any event, if the division of shares is to be by reference to the total costs incurred in purchase (and not just the purchase price), the relevant figures may not be known at the time of completion.

(b) Registered land

The transfer to two or more purchasers will be in form TRI and if **2–006** the transferees execute it they will declare that they hold the property either as tenants in common or alternatively upon the terms of a declaration of trust to be executed immediately thereafter. The Registrar will automatically enter a restriction in Form A to the effect that no disposition by a sole proprietor of the land (not being a trust corporation) under which capital money arises is to be registered unless authorised by an order of the court. This entry is obligatory where the survivor of registered joint proprietors will not be able to give a valid receipt for capital monies (Land Registration Act 2002, s.44(1), Land Registration Rules 2003, r.95(2) and Form A, Sch.4). No fee is payable in respect of the entry of this restriction.

3. THE CONTENTS OF THE DECLARATION

The precedents that follow in this chapter concentrate on the **2–007** percentage interests of the parties. However, there is no reason why the declaration should not contain (if applicable) provisions as to the subjects set out below.

(a) Outgoings

It should be agreed as to whether or not a party who pays **2–008** outgoings such as insurance, chief rent, etc. should be reimbursed. The practical view is that the occupier of the property should pay these.

(b) Repairs

It should be agreed as to whether or not one party has the obligation to see to repairs and either to pay the costs, or perhaps receive reimbursement as to half (or whatever agreed proportion) out of the proceeds of sale before division.

(c) Power of sale

2–009   Land held by two or more persons is held upon a trust of land (Law of Property Act 1925, s.36 and see p.4 above). As trustees of land they have the powers of an absolute owner including a power of sale (Trusts of Land and Appointment of Trustees Act 1996 s.6(1)). Under s.8 Trusts of Land and Appointment of Trustees Act it is possible for a declaration of trust to contain provisions limiting the trustees powers. If, therefore, there are to be restrictions, say, as to when a sale is to take place, these should be contained in the declaration of trust (see Precedents 9 or 10). It will be appreciated that while such an agreement may be binding *inter partes*, it will not bind a mortgagee who will only have been concerned with the legal estate.

   If the powers of trustees of land to deal with the property are to be limited as permitted by s.8 above for example if consents to sale or exercise of other powers are required, that limitation must be reflected by entry of a restriction in form B in the case of registered land (Land Registration Rules 2003 r.94(4) and Form B Sch.4). This restriction is in addition to the usual Form A restriction. The prescribed form B restriction simply requires a statutory declaration by the trustees or, more usually, a certificate by the trustees' conveyancer that the provisions of the trust have been complied with. Application is made on Form RX1, the fee payable being £40 (see Precedent 9A).

(d) Appointment of new trustees

Unless alternative provision is made in the declaration, on the death of one of two tenants in common the survivor will have the power to appoint a new trustee under Trustee Act 1925, s.36. The parties should consider whether they would prefer a replacement trustee to be appointed by the personal representatives of the deceased party or by the survivor with the consent of such personal representatives. If either of these courses is followed the parties should apply to register a voluntary restriction in form Q in the case of registered land,using Form RX1, the fee payable being £40 (see Prededent 6A).

(e) Mortgage payments

It should be considered who is to be responsible for paying these **2–010** and whether or not there is to be any form of reimbursement on sale. Given the different forms of mortgages, this can present real difficulty and the majority of cohabitees, for instance, will accept that either the mortgage is to be paid equally, or that one of them is entitled to a greater percentage of the proceeds of sale (such percentage being fixed at the outset), given the fact that he or she is to be paying the mortgage (or most of it). This is probably preferable to keeping detailed accounts and records. However, the question of the mortgage must be thought about as should the entitlement to any life policy or other investment taken out in connection therewith.

Where property is purchased by several people, they may have effected separate borrowing arrangements. Whilst a mortgagee will take a legal charge over the property, the owners will wish to cover this position as between themselves.

It will be appreciated that an indemnity will be worthless if the party giving it has no assets or income stream to back it up.

It seems to be common practice for instance for medical **2–011** practitioners to purchase premises, and obviously from time to time there are changes in the medical partnership, with a new partner often purchasing a retiring partner's share in the premises. It is usual for the same bank to finance each of the partners, taking a charge on the surgery premises to secure those borrowings. It is important therefore, between themselves that the partners create cross-indemnities (see Precedent 7).

Similarly, a husband may wish to borrow monies on the security of a second mortgage on the house owned by himself and his wife for the purposes of his business. Whilst they are both primarily liable to the mortgagee in respect of such mortgage, the wife may wish to protect her interest in the dwellinghouse so far as she can. She should certainly insist on the lender agreeing a limit to the amount of borrowing being charged on the property and should obtain an indemnity from the husband in respect of the second mortgage (see Precedent 5).

4. DEATH OF A TENANT IN COMMON

2–012 Where the death of a tenant in common occurs so that the legal title stands in the name of one person alone, it is necessary to appoint a further trustee of the legal estate so that a good receipt for capital monies is obtained by any purchaser (Law of Property Act 1925, s.27(2) as amended by Trusts of Land and Appointment of Trustees Act 1996, Sch.3, para.4(1),(8)(b) and indeed, in the case of registered land, so that a transfer will be registered. (see restriction above, p.13).

The original declaration of trust may specify that the power of appointment of a new trustee on the death of one of the trustees is vested in the personal representatives of that trustee or requires the consent of those personal representatives.

Subject to the provisions of the original declaration of trust the Trustee Act 1925, s.36 allows a surviving trustee to appoint a new trustee. If it is not envisaged that the property will be sold until after the death of the surviving tenant in common it might be prudent to appoint two new trustees so that they are in place at the time of the second death (see Precedents 3A and 3B).

5. CONTINUING RESIDENCE FOR THE SURVIVOR

2–013 Where two people (not husband and wife) live together they may feel that whilst they would like their entitlements in the jointly owned property to pass to their own families eventually, they would wish their companion to have the right to remain in the property for so long as he or she wishes. Precedent 10 is designed to cover such a situation and to allow a change of residence should this be required.

It is envisaged that the original tenants in common will be the trustees. On the death of one of them his personal representatives have the power of appointing a replacement trustee.

It will be observed (see p.44) that sale is to take place on the happening of a specified event, and that one of these is cohabitation of the survivor with another. Cohabitation is a difficult factual situation to define; this event is included so as to put the draftsman on notice that he should discuss the position with his clients.

The precedent can be adapted to a situation where there is a mortgage or no mortgage. The question of life policies would have to be considered separately.

6. Steps to be Taken

(a) Stamp Duty Land Tax

The declarations of trust will not in general attract SDLT or **2–014** require a self certificate as they do not effect any transfer. However the transfer on appointment of new trustees (Prededent 3B), although exempt from SDLT under Finance Act 2003, s.49, Sch.3 para.1 as there is no chargeable consideration, will require a self certificate in form SDLT 60. As the declaration in Precedent 8 in effect constitutes a sale, SDLT will be payable and a land transaction return must be made.

(b) Copies

It is obviously prudent that each tenant in common has a copy of the declaration of trust to prove his entitlement.

PRECEDENTS

2–015 Precedent 1—Property purchased by two persons as tenants in common. Straightforward agreement on division of sale proceeds in percentage shares. No mortgage.

THIS DECLARATION OF TRUST is made this   day of
      200
BETWEEN   (1)   [X]   of   [address]   and   (2)   [Y]
of   [address]

WHEREAS:

(A) By a Conveyance/Transfer dated   the property
("the Property") details of which are contained in the Schedule
hereto was conveyed/transferred to [X] and [Y] to be held by them
[unregistered land] as tenants in common
or [registered land] subject to the usual joint proprietorship
restriction

(B) The parties make this Declaration to set out their respective
interests in the Property and its proceeds of sale and net rents and
profits thereof until sale

NOW THIS DEED WITNESSES as follows:

1 The parties hereto DECLARE that they hold the Property on a
trust of land

2 The parties hereto DECLARE that they hold the Property and
its proceeds of sale (after deducting therefrom the costs of sale)
and the net rents and profits until sale UPON TRUST for
themselves as tenants in common:

  (a) as to [60%] for X absolutely

  (b) as to [40%] for Y absolutely

IN WITNESS whereof this Declaration has been duly executed
the day and year before written

SCHEDULE

[unregistered land—brief description]

[registered land—Title No
            —Address]

SIGNED AND DELIVERED as a
Deed by [X] in the presence of:

SIGNED AND DELIVERED as a
Deed by [Y] in the presence of:

Precedent 2—Property purchased by two persons as tenants in common: details of purchase price and costs set out: division by reference to those. No mortgage.

2–016 THIS DECLARATION OF TRUST [*continue as Precedent 1*]

WHEREAS:

(A) [As Precedent 1]

(B) [As Precedent 1] [continue by reference to its purchase price and the costs of purchase thereof]

NOW IT IS HEREBY DECLARED as follows:

1 The purchase price of the Property and the costs of purchase were as follows:

> Purchase price
>
> Stamp Duty
>
> Surveyors Costs
>
> H.M. Land Registry fees
>
> Other costs fees and disbursements

_____

Total £

_____

2 It is agreed that X contributed £   to the total set out in Clause 1 hereof and Y contributed the balance of £

3 The parties hereto DECLARE that they hold the Property on a trust of land

4. The parties hereto DECLARE that they hold the Property and its proceeds of sale (after deducting therefrom the costs of sale) and the net rents and profits until sale UPON TRUST for themselves as tenants in common:

(a) as to $\frac{\text{X's contribution}}{\text{total}}$ % for X absolutely

(b) as to $\frac{\text{Y's contribution}}{\text{total}}$ % for Y absolutely

IN WITNESS etc

SCHEDULE
[see Precedent 1]

Attestation—[*as Precedent 1*]

Precedent 3A—Deed of appointment of new trustees following death of one tenant in common. Unregistered land.

2–017 THIS DEED OF APPOINTMENT is made this   day of
200   BETWEEN (1) [Y] of
[address] ("the Appointor") and (2) [A] of   [address]
and [B] of   [address] ("the New Trustees")

WHEREAS:

(A) By a Conveyance ("the Conveyance") dated   and made
between (1) [vendors to X and Y] and (2) [X] and the Appointor
the freehold property ("the Property") details of which are
contained in the Schedule was conveyed to [X] and the Appointor
in fee simple and is held by them as trustees of land.

(B) [X] and the Appointor hold the Property and its net proceeds
of sale and the net income until sale upon trust for themselves as
tenants in common

(C) [X] died on [date]

(D) The Appointor wishes to appoint the New Trustees to be
trustees of the trusts of the Conveyance in place of [X]

NOW THIS DEED WITNESSES that in exercise of the statutory
power and of every other power him enabling the Appointor
HEREBY APPOINTS the New Trustees to be trustees of the
trusts of the Conveyance jointly with the Appointor and in place
of [X]

IN WITNESS whereof this Deed has been duly executed the
day and year before written

SCHEDULE

[Description of Property]

Attestation—[as Precedent 1]

Note: A memorandum should be placed on the conveyance
stating the names of the new trustees following the appointment.

Precedent 3B—Registered land—transfer on appointment of new trustees

| Transfer of whole of registered title(s) | Land Registry | **TR1** |

If you need more room than is provided for in this panel, use continuation sheet CS and attach to this form.

---

1. Stamp Duty

Place "X" in the appropriate box or boxes and complete the appropriate certificate.

☐ It is certified that this instrument falls within category ☐ in the Schedule to the Stamp Duty (Exempt Instruments) Regulations 1987

☐ It is certified that the transaction effected does not form part of a larger transaction or of a series of transactions in respect of which the amount or value or the aggregate amount or value

of the consideration exceeds the sum of | £ |

☐ It is certified that this is an instrument on which stamp duty is not chargeable by virtue of the provisions of section 92 of the Finance Act 2001

---

2. Title Number(s) of the Property *Leave blank if not yet registered.*

[TITLE NUMBER]

---

3. Property

[ADDRESS]

---

4. Date

---

5. Transferor *Give full names and company's registered number if any.*
[Y] of [ADDRESS] (SURVIVING TENANT IN COMMON)

---

6. Transferee **for entry on the register** *Give full name(s) and company's registered number if any: for Scottish companies use an SC prefix and for limited partnerships use the OC prefix before the registered number, if any. For foreign companies give territory in which incorporated.*
[Y] AND [A] AND [B]
(NEW TRUSTEES)

Unless otherwise arranged with Land Registry headquarters, a certified copy of the Transferee's constitution (in English or Welsh) will be required if it is a body corporate but is not a company registered in England and Wales or Scotland under the Companies Acts.

---

7. Transferee's intended **address(es) for service (including postcode) for entry on the register** *You may give up to three addresses for service **one** of which **must** be a postal address but does not have to be within the UK. The other addresses can be any combination of a postal address, a box number at a UK document exchange or an electronic address.*

[ADDRESSES]

---

8. The Transferor transfers the property to the Transferee.

---

9. Consideration *Place "X" in the appropriate box. State clearly the currency unit if other than sterling. If none of the boxes applies, insert an appropriate memorandum in the additional provisions panel.*

☐ The Transferor has received from the Transferee for the Property the sum of *In words and figures.*

☐ *Insert other receipt as appropriate.*

☒ The transfer is not for money or anything which has a monetary value

10. The Transferor transfers with *Place "X" in the appropriate box and add any modifications.*

☐ full title guarantee   ☒ limited title guarantee

---

11. Declaration of trust *Where there is more than one Transferee, place "X" in the appropriate box.*

☐ The Transferees are to hold the Property on trust for themselves as joint tenants

☒ The Transferees are to hold the Property on trust for themselves as tenants in common in equal shares [OR AS APPROPRIATE]

☐ The Transferees are to hold the property *Complete as necessary.*

---

12. Additional provisions *Insert here any required or permitted statements, certificates or applications and any agreed covenants, declarations, etc.*

This transfer is made for the purpose of giving effect to the appointment of new trustees X having died   on [   ]

---

13. Execution   *The Transferor must execute this transfer as a deed using the space below. If there is more than one Transferor, all must execute. Forms of execution are given in Schedule 9 to the Land Registration Rules 2003. If the transfer contains Transferee's covenants or declarations or contains an application by the Transferee (e.g. for a restriction), it must also be executed by the Transferees (all of them if there is more than one).*

Signed as a deed by (enter full name of individual) in the presence of:

> Signature
>
>   **Y**

Signature of Witness . . . .

     Name (in BLOCK CAPITALS). . . . .

     Address. . . . .

Signed as a deed by (enter full name of individual) in the presence of:

> Signature
>
>   **A**

     Signature of Witness . . . .

     Name (in BLOCK CAPITALS). . . . .

     Address. . . . .

**Continuation sheet
for use with
application and
disposition forms**

Land Registry

CS

1. Continued from Form	TRI	Title number(s)	[TITLE NUMBER]

2. *Before each continuation, state panel to be continued, e.g. "Panel 12 continued".*

Panel 13 continued

**Signed as a deed by (enter full name
of individual) in the presence of:**

Signature

B

Signature of Witness...

Name (in BLOCK CAPITALS)....................................

Address...

Continuation sheet [ ] **of** [ ]
*(Insert sheet number and total number of continuation
sheets e.g. "sheet 1 of 3")*
Crown copyright (ref:LR/HQ/CD-ROM 6/03

Note: The application to register the transfer should be accompanied by evidence of the death of any former trustee.

Precedent 4—Property purchased by two persons as tenants in common. Mortgage. Division in percentage shares.

2–019 THIS DECLARATION OF TRUST is made this   day of 200
BETWEEN   (1)   [X]   of   [*address*]   and   (2)   [Y] of   [*address*]

WHEREAS:

(A) [As Precedent 1]

(B) By a Mortgage ("the Mortgage") dated   made between (1) the Parties hereto and (2) the [Building Society] the Property was charged to the [Building Society] to secure the sum of £

(C) The purchase price of the Property and the costs of purchase were provided as to £   by [X] and £   by [Y] and £   by the Mortgage.

(D) The parties make this Declaration to set out their respective interests in the Property and its proceeds of sale and net rents and profits thereof until sale

NOW THIS DEED WITNESSES as follows:

1 The parties hereto DECLARE that they hold the Property on a trust of land.

2 The parties hereto DECLARE that they hold the Property and its proceeds of sale (after discharging the mortgage and deducting therefrom the costs of sale) and the net rents and profits until sale UPON TRUST for themselves as tenants in common:

    (a) as to [%] for X absolutely

    (b) as to [%] for Y absolutely

3 In this deed the expression "the Mortgage" shall include any future substitution for the Mortgage or addition thereto

    IN WITNESS etc

SCHEDULE

[see Precedent 1]

Attestation—*[as Precedent 1]*

Precedent 5—Property held by two persons as tenants in common subject to first mortgage. One joint owner wishing to raise additional money by way of second mortgage and indemnifying the other. Assumes plenty of equity in the property.

2–020 THIS DECLARATION OF TRUST is made this   day of 200

BETWEEN (1) [X] of   [*address*] and (2) [Y] of   [*address*]

WHEREAS:

(A) [as Precedent 1]

(B) By a Mortgage ("the Mortgage") dated   and made between (1) the Parties hereto and (2) the [Building Society] the Property was charged to the [Building Society] to secure the sum of £

(C) X is indebted to [*Bank*] and Y has agreed to execute a second mortgage ("the Second Mortgage") with X in favour of [*Bank*] provided that she is indemnified as herein set out

(D) The parties make this Declaration to set out their respective interests in the Property and its proceeds of sale and net rents and profits thereof until sale

NOW THIS DEED WITNESSES as follows:

1 X and Y DECLARE that they hold the Property on a trust of land

2 X and Y DECLARE that they hold the Property and its proceeds of sale (after discharging the Mortgage and the Second Mortgage and deducting therefrom the costs of sale) and the net rents and profits until sale UPON TRUST for themselves as tenants in common:

   (a) to pay Y a sum equal to the sum required to discharge the second mortgage in favour of [*Bank*]

   (b) to hold the balance:

   — as to [%] for X

   — as to [%] for Y

3 X covenants with Y to pay all payments required in connection with the Second Morgage and to indemnify Y and keep her indemnified accordingly

IN WITNESS etc

SCHEDULE

[see Precedent 1]

Attestation—[as Precedent 1]

Precedent 6—Property held by trustees (X and Y) upon trust for X, Y and Z in unequal shares. No mortgage.

2–021 THIS DECLARATION OF TRUST is made this   day of   200

BETWEEN   (1)   [X]   of   [address]   and   [Y] of   [address] ("the Trustees") which expression shall mean the trustee or trustees for the time being hereof) and (2) [Z] of   [address]

WHEREAS:

(A) [as Precedent 1]

(B) The Trustees make this Declaration to set out the respective interests of [X] [Y] and [Z] in the Property and its proceeds of sale and net rents and profits thereof until sale and [Z] has joined in the Declaration to confirm his interest

NOW THIS DEED WITNESSES as follows:

1 The Trustees DECLARE that they hold the Property on a trust of land

2 The Trustees DECLARE that they hold the Property and its proceeds of sale (after deducting therefrom the costs of sale) and the net rents and profits until sale UPON TRUST for themselves and Z as tenants in common

  (a) as to [40%] for X absolutely

  (b) as to [40%] for Y absolutely

  (c) as to [20%] for Z absolutely

3 The power of appointing new or additional trustees of this Declaration and of the Conveyance/Property shall be vested in X Y and Z or their respective personal representatives

  IN WITNESS etc

SCHEDULE

[see Precedent 1]

Attestation—*[as Precedent 1]*

Note: Application to be made in form RX1 to enter a voluntary restriction in respect of the power of appointing new trustees of registered land.

Precedent 6A—Registered land—Application to register a form Q restriction to reflect limitations on appointment of trustees in Precedent 6

Application to enter a restriction	Land Registry	**RX1**

If you need more room than is provided for in a panel, use continuation sheet CS and attach to this form.

---

1. Administrative area and postcode if known   [AREA]

2. Title number(s) [TITLE NUMBER]

---

3. If you have already made this application by **outline application,** insert reference number:

---

4. Property *Insert address or other description.*
[ADDRESS]
The restriction applied for is to affect *Place "X" in the appropriate box and complete as necessary.*

☒ the whole of each registered estate

☐ the part(s) of the registered estate(s) shown on the attached plan by *State reference e.g. "edged red".*

☐ the registered charge(s) dated   in favour of
                                   referred to in the Charges Register

---

5. Application and fee *A fee calculator for all types of applications can be found on Land Registry's website at www.landregistry.gov.uk/fees*

Restriction   Fee paid £40

Fee payment method: *Place "X" in the appropriate box.*

I wish to pay the appropriate fee payable under the current Land Registration Fee Order:

☐ by cheque or postal order, amount £_____ made payable to "Land Registry".

☐ by Direct Debit under an authorised agreement with Land Registry.

FOR OFFICIAL USE ONLY
Record of fee paid

Particulars of under/over payment

Fees debited £

Reference number

---

6. Documents lodged with this application *If this application is accompanied by either Form AP1 or FR1 please only complete the corresponding panel on Form AP1 or DL. Number the documents in sequence; copies should also be numbered and listed as separate documents, alternatively you may prefer to use Form DL. If you supply the original document and a certified copy, we shall assume that you request the return of the original; if a certified copy is not supplied, we may retain the original document and it may be destroyed.*

Declaration of trust dated [   ] made between [X] and [Y] and certified copy of the same

---

7. The applicant is: *Please provide the full name of the person applying for the restriction.*
   [X] and [Y]

The application has been lodged by:
Land Registry Key No. (if appropriate)
Name (if different from the applicant)
Address/DX No.   [ADDRESS]

Reference
E-mail

Telephone No.	Fax No.

FOR OFFICIAL USE ONLY
Codes
Dealing

Status

8. Where you would like us to deal with someone else *We shall deal only with the applicant, or the person lodging the application if different, unless you place "X" against one or more of the statements below and give the necessary details.*

☐ Send title information document to the person shown below

☐ Raise any requisitions or queries with the person shown below

☐ Return original documents lodged with this form (see note in panel 6) to the person shown below
If this applies only to certain documents, please specify.

Name
Address/DX No.

Reference
E-mail

Telephone No.	Fax No.

9. Entitlement to apply for a restriction *Place "X" in the appropriate box.*

☒ The applicant is the registered proprietor of the registered estate/charge referred to in panel 4.

☐ The applicant is the person **entitled** to be registered as proprietor of the registered estate/charge referred to in panel 4. **Complete panel 12.**

☐ The consent of the registered proprietor of the registered estate/charge referred to in panel 4 accompanies this application or the applicant's conveyancer certifies that he holds this consent. **Complete panel 11.**

☐ The consent of the person **entitled** to be registered as proprietor of the registered estate/charge referred to in panel 4 accompanies this application or the applicant's conveyancer certifies that he holds this consent. **Complete panels 11 and 12.**

☐ Evidence that the applicant has sufficient interest in the making of the entry of the restriction applied for in panel 10 accompanies this application. **Complete panel 13.**

10. The applicant applies to enter the following restriction against the registered estate/charge referred to in panel 4: *Please set out the form of restriction required. Schedule 4 to the Land Registration Rules 2003 contains standard forms of restrictions. Use this form to apply for a standard form of restriction (as set out in Schedule 4 to the Land Registration Rules 2003) or, where appropriate, a restriction in another form. If the restriction is not a standard form of restriction, the registrar must be satisfied that the terms of the proposed restriction are reasonable and that applying the proposed restriction would be straightforward and not place an unreasonable burden on him. If the restriction requires notice to be given to a person, requires a person's consent or certificate or is a standard form restriction that refers to a named person, include that person's address for service.*

No disposition of the registered estate by the proprieter of the registered estate is to be registered after the death of either [X] or [Y] without the written consent of the personal representatives of the deceased.

11. Evidence of consent *Please complete this panel if instructed to do so in panel 9. Place "X" in the appropriate box.*

☐ The [registered proprietor of][person entitled to be registered as the proprietor of] the registered estate/charge referred to in panel 4 consents to the entry of the restriction and that person or their conveyancer has completed panel 15.

☐ I am the applicant's conveyancer and certify that I hold the consent referred to in panel 9.

☐ The consent referred to in panel 9 is contained on page ____ of the document numbered ____ referred to in [panel 6][Form AP1][Form DL].

12. Evidence of entitlement to be registered as proprietor *Please complete this panel if instructed to do so in panel 9. Place "X" in the appropriate box.*

☐ I am the applicant's conveyancer and certify that I am satisfied that the applicant/person consenting to this application is entitled to be registered as proprietor and that I hold the originals of the documents that contain evidence of that person's entitlement, or an application for registration of that person as proprietor is pending at Land Registry.

☐ Evidence that the applicant/person consenting to this application is entitled to be registered as proprietor is contained in the document(s) numbered ____ referred to in [panel 6][Form AP1][Form DL].

13. Evidence that the applicant has sufficient interest *Please complete this panel if instructed to do so in panel 9.*

State brief details of the applicant's interest in the making of the entry of the restriction applied for in panel 10.

Evidence of this interest is contained in the document(s) numbered referred to in [panel 6] [Form AP1][Form DL].

14. Signature of applicant

or their conveyancer _____ **Date** _____

15. Consent
Consent to the entry of the restriction specified in panel 10 is given by:

Names BLOCK LETTERS   **Signatures**

1.   1.

2.   2.

3.   3.

© Crown copyright (ref: LR/HQ) 6/03

Precedent 7—Property held by four trustees for themselves equally but charged to secure the borrowings of three of them.

THIS DECLARATION OF TRUST is made this   day 2–022
of   200
BETWEEN   (1) [A]   of   [address]   ("A")   (2)   [B]
of   [address] ("B") (3) [C] of   [address] ("C")
and (4) [D]   of [address] (D)

WHEREAS:

(A) [as Precedent 6]

(B) The Property is charged to [Bank] by way of three Legal Charges to secure sums advanced respectively to [A] [B] and [D] who have differing obligations to the [Bank]

(C) The parties make this Declaration to set out their respective interests in the Property and to give the indemnities herein contained

NOW THIS DEED WITNESSES as follows:

1 The parties hereto DECLARE that they hold the Property on a trust of land

2 The parties hereto DECLARE that they hold the Property and its proceeds of sale (after deducting therefrom the costs of sale) and the net rents and profits until sale UPON TRUST for themselves as tenants in common

  (a) as to 25% thereof for [A]

  (b) as to 25% thereof for [B]

  (c) as to 25% thereof for [C]

  (d) as to 25% thereof for [D]

2 Although as between the parties hereto and [Bank] each of the parties is liable to the [Bank] in respect of any obligations under the said Legal Charges IT IS HEREBY AGREED and each party hereto covenants with each of the other parties to pay and discharge his or her respective obligations to the [Bank] and to keep the other parties and each of them and their respective estates indemnified in respect of any liability they or any of them

might suffer by failure on his or her part to discharge such obligations and each party hereto hereby charges his or her interest in the Property to the others to secure any monies which become due under this indemnity

IN WITNESS etc

SCHEDULE

[see Precedent 1]

Attestation—*[as Precedent 1]*

Precedent 8—Property held by four persons as tenants in common in equal shares. Now held for five persons equally by reason of sale.

THIS DECLARATION OF TRUST is made this   day **2–023**
of   200
BETWEEN   (1)   [A]   of   [address]   [B]
of   [address]   [C]   of   [address]   and   [D]
of   [address]   ("the   Trustees")   and   (2)   [E]
of   [address] ("the New Partner")

WHEREAS:

(A) By a Conveyance/Transfer dated   the property
("the Property") details of which are contained in the Schedule hereto was conveyed/transferred to the Trustees to be held by them
[unregistered land] as tenants in common in equal shares
or [registered land] subject to the usual joint proprietorship restriction and declared by them in a Declaration of Trust dated   to be held for them as tenants in common in equal shares

(B) The New Partner having agreed to pay the sum of £   to the Trustees to be received by them in equal shares it is agreed that on receipt the Property will thenceforth be held by the Trustees as to one fifth for each of themselves and the New Partner

NOW THIS DEED WITNESSES as follows:

1 In consideration of the sum of £   paid to the Trustees in equal shares (receipt of which the Trustees hereby acknowledge) the Trustees DECLARE that henceforth they will hold the Property on a trust of land and that they will hold the Property and its net proceeds of sale and the net rents and profits thereof until sale UPON TRUST as to one fifth for each of themselves and the New Partner as tenants in common and that the trusts of the Conveyance/Declaration of Trust before referred to shall be varied accordingly

2 The New Partner covenants with the Trustees that henceforth he will pay one fifth of the outgoings of the Property and will indemnify the Trustees in respect of his one fifth share thereof

[3 It is hereby certified that the transaction hereby effected does not form part of a larger transaction or of a series of transactions in respect of which the amount or value or the aggregate amount of value of the consideration exceeds [£60,000] [£250,000] or [£500,000] (as appropriate)

IN WITNESS etc

SCHEDULE

[see *Precedent 1*]

Attestation—[*as Precedent 1*]

Precedent 9—Property purchased by daughter (X) son-in-law (Y) and mother-in-law (A), X and Y holding legal title as joint tenants and mortgaging property, indemnity to mother-in-law.

THIS DECLARATION OF TRUST is made this   day of **2–024**
    200

BETWEEN (1) [X] and [Y] both of   [address] ("the Trustees") and (2) [A] of   [address] ("Mrs A")

WHEREAS:

(A) By a Conveyance/Transfer dated   the property ("the Property") details of which are contained in the Schedule hereto was conveyed/transferred to the Trustees in fee simple in consideration of the sum of [£90,000]

(B) By a mortgage ("the Mortgage") dated   made between (1) the Trustees and (2) [Building Society] the Property was charged to the [Building Society] to secure the sum of £

(C) The purchase price of the Property and the costs of purchase were [£92,000] and were provided as follows:

The Trustees (including the sum borrowed under the Mortgage)	[62,000]
[Mrs A]	[30,000]
	[£92,000]

(D) The Trustees and Mrs A agree that the Trustees hold the Property upon the trusts herein set out

NOW THIS DEED WITNESSES as follows:

1 The Trustees shall hold the Property on a trust of land

2 The Trustees shall hold the Property and the proceeds of sale (after deducting therefrom the costs of sale) and the net rents and profits until sale UPON TRUST for themselves and Mrs A as tenants in common

(a) as to $\frac{(62,000)}{(92,000)}$ % for X and Y ("X and Y's share")

(b) as to $\frac{(30,000)}{(92,000)}$ % for Mrs A

3 As between themselves X and Y shall hold X and Y's Share in the Property as beneficial joint tenants

4 The Trustees hereby agree that they will not exercise their statutory power of sale of the Property without the written consent of [Mrs. A] during her lifetime [so long as it remains her principal residence]

5(a) X and Y hereby covenant with [Mrs A] (and for the benefit of her personal representatives) that they will pay all payments required under the Mortgage and that they will indemnify and keep indemnified [Mrs A] and her personal representatives against all costs liabilities and claims in respect of the Mortgage
(b) X and Y further covenant with [Mrs A] and her personal representatives that on any sale of the Property they will discharge all monies owing under the Mortgage and all costs liabilities and claims in respect thereof out of the X and Y's Share

6 The power of appointing new or additional Trustees of this Declaration and of the Conveyance/Property is vested in X Y and [Mrs A] jointly or the survivor or survivors of them

7 Every reference in this Declaration to "the Trustees" shall mean and include the trustee or trustees for the time being hereof
    IN WITNESS etc

SCHEDULE

[see Precedent 1]

Attestation—*[as Precedent 1]*

Note: Application to be made on Form RX1 to enter Form B restriction to effect limitation on power of sale if registered land.

Precedent 9A—Application by proprieter to register a form B restriction under LRR 2003 Rule 94(4)

Application to enter a restriction	**Land Registry**	**RX1**

If you need more room than is provided for in a panel, use continuation sheet CS and attach to this form.

1. Administrative area and postcode if known   [AREA]

2. Title number(s) [TITLE NUMBER]

3. If you have already made this application by **outline application,** insert reference number:

4. Property *Insert address or other description.*
[ADDRESS]

The restriction applied for is to affect Place "X" in the appropriate box and complete as necessary.

☒ the whole of each registered estate

☐ the part(s) of the registered estate(s) shown on the attached plan by *State reference e.g. "edged red".*

☐ the registered charge(s) dated   in favour of
referred to in the Charges Register

5. Application and fee *A fee calculator for all types of applications can be found on Land Registry's website at www.landregistry.gov.uk/fees*

Restriction   Fee paid £40

Fee payment method: *Place "X" in the appropriate box.*

I wish to pay the appropriate fee payable under the current Land Registration Fee Order:

☐ by cheque or postal order, amount £_____ made payable to "Land Registry".

☐ by Direct Debit under an authorised agreement with Land Registry.

FOR OFFICIAL USE ONLY
Record of fee paid

Particulars of under/over payment

Fees debited £

Reference number

6. Documents lodged with this application *If this application is accompanied by either Form AP1 or FR1 please only complete the corresponding panel on Form AP1 or DL. Number the documents in sequence; copies should also be numbered and listed as separate documents, alternatively you may prefer to use Form DL. If you supply the original document and a certified copy, we shall assume that you request the return of the original; if a certified copy is not supplied, we may retain the original document and it may be destroyed.*

Declaration of trust dated [   ] made between [X] and [Y] and certified copy of the same

7. The applicant is: *Please provide the full name of the person applying for the restriction.*
    X (LEGAL OWNER)

The application has been lodged by:
Land Registry Key No. (if appropriate)
Name (if different from the applicant)
Address/DX No.   [ADDRESS]

Reference
E-mail

FOR OFFICIAL USE ONLY
Codes
Dealing

Status

Telephone No.	Fax No.

8. **Where you would like us to deal with someone else** *We shall deal only with the applicant, or the person lodging the application if different, unless you place "X" against one or more of the statements below and give the necessary details.*

☐ Send title information document to the person shown below

☐ Raise any requisitions or queries with the person shown below

☐ Return original documents lodged with this form (see note in panel 6) to the person shown below
If this applies only to certain documents, please specify.

Name
Address/DX No.

Reference
E-mail

Telephone No.	Fax No.

9. **Entitlement to apply for a restriction** *Place "X" in the appropriate box.*

☒ The applicant is the registered proprietor of the registered estate/charge referred to in panel 4.

☐ The applicant is the person **entitled** to be registered as proprietor of the registered estate/charge referred to in panel 4. **Complete panel 12.**

☐ The consent of the registered proprietor of the registered estate/charge referred to in panel 4 accompanies this application or the applicant's conveyancer certifies that he holds this consent. **Complete panel 11.**

☐ The consent of the person **entitled** to be registered as proprietor of the registered estate/charge referred to in panel 4 accompanies this application or the applicant's conveyancer certifies that he holds this consent. **Complete panels 11 and 12.**

☐ Evidence that the applicant has sufficient interest in the making of the entry of the restriction applied for in panel 10 accompanies this application. **Complete panel 13.**

10. **The applicant applies to enter the following restriction against the registered estate/charge referred to in panel 4:** *Please set out the form of restriction required. Schedule 4 to the Land Registration Rules 2003 contains standard forms of restrictions. Use this form to apply for a standard form of restriction (as set out in Schedule 4 to the Land Registration Rules 2003) or, where appropriate, a restriction in another form. If the restriction is not a standard form of restriction, the registrar must be satisfied that the terms of the proposed restriction are reasonable and that applying the proposed restriction would be straightforward and not place an unreasonable burden on him. If the restriction requires notice to be given to a person, requires a person's consent or certificate or is a standard form restriction that refers to a named person, include that person's address for service.*

No disposition by the proprieters of the registered estate is to be registered unless they make a statutory declaration or their conveyancer gives a certificate that the disposition is in accordance with a Declaration of Trust dated [   ] and made by [X] of [ADDRESS] and [Y] of [ADDRESS] or some variation thereof referred to in the declaration or certificate.

11. Evidence of consent *Please complete this panel if instructed to do so in panel 9. Place "X" in the appropriate box.*

☐ The [registered proprietor of][person entitled to be registered as the proprietor of] the registered estate/charge referred to in panel 4 consents to the entry of the restriction and that person or their conveyancer has completed panel 15.

☐ I am the applicant's conveyancer and certify that I hold the consent referred to in panel 9.

☐ The consent referred to in panel 9 is contained on page ____ of the document numbered ____ referred to in [panel 6][Form AP1][Form DL].

12. Evidence of entitlement to be registered as proprietor *Please complete this panel if instructed to do so in panel 9. Place "X" in the appropriate box.*

☐ I am the applicant's conveyancer and certify that I am satisfied that the applicant/person consenting to this application is entitled to be registered as proprietor and that I hold the originals of the documents that contain evidence of that person's entitlement, or an application for registration of that person as proprietor is pending at Land Registry.

☐ Evidence that the applicant/person consenting to this application is entitled to be registered as proprietor is contained in the document(s) numbered ____ referred to in [panel 6][Form AP1][Form DL].

13. Evidence that the applicant has sufficient interest *Please complete this panel if instructed to do so in panel 9.*

State brief details of the applicant's interest in the making of the entry of the restriction applied for in panel 10.

Evidence of this interest is contained in the document(s) numbered referred to in [panel 6] [Form AP1][Form DL].

14. Signature of applicant

or their conveyancer _____ **Date** _____

15. Consent
Consent to the entry of the restriction specified in panel 10 is given by:

Names BLOCK LETTERS   **Signatures**

1.   1.

2.   2.

3.   3.

Precedent 10—Property held by two persons as tenants in common, contribution to purchase price specified. Right of survivor to continue to reside and change dwelling. Can be applied to mortgage or non-mortgage situation.

2–025 THIS DECLARATION OF TRUST is made the   day of 200

BY   (1)   [X]   of   [address]   ("X")   and   [Y] of   [address]   ("Y")   (together   called   "the   Trustees" which expression shall include all other the trustee or trustees for the time being hereof)

WHEREAS:

(A) By a Conveyance/Transfer dated   the property ("the Property") details of which are contained in the Schedule hereto ("the Property") was conveyed/transferred to the Trustees to be held by them
[unregistered land] as tenants in common or subject to the usual joint proprietorship [registered land] restriction

[(B) By a mortgage ("the Mortgage") dated   and made between (1) the Trustees and (2) [Building Society] the Property was charged to [Building Society] to secure the sum of £   ]

(C) or (B) The Trustees make this Declaration to set out their respective interests in the Property by reference to its purchase price and the costs of purchase thereof and the trusts powers and provisions subject to which the Property is held

NOW IT IS HEREBY DECLARED as follows:

1 The following expressions shall have the following meanings:

(a) "the dwelling" shall mean ALL THAT the Property and any house bungalow flat or maisonette purchased by the Trustees in accordance with the provisions hereof in substitution for the Property

(b) "the residing party" shall mean such of X or Y as shall reside or continue to reside in the dwelling after the death of the first to die of X or Y

(c) "the specified events" shall mean:

(i) the death of the survivor of X and Y
(ii) the marriage or re-marriage of either X or Y after the death of the first to die of X or Y

[(iii) the cohabitation of the survivor with any other person]

whichever shall first occur

(d) "the net proceeds of sale" shall mean the proceeds of sale of the dwelling after payment of the costs of sale [and repayment of the Mortgage]

2 The purchase price of the Property and the costs of purchase were as follows:

Purchase Price

Inland Revenue Stamp Duty

Surveyors fees

H.M. Land Registry fees

Legal fees

Other costs fees and disbursements

_____

Total £

_____

3 It is agreed that X contributed £   to the Total set out in Clause 2 hereof and Y contributed £   [and the balance was provided by the Mortgage]

4 The Trustees shall hold the dwelling as trustees of land.

5(a) The Trustees may permit the residing party to reside in and continue to reside in the dwelling without payment therefore made by the residing party to the Trustees and provided none of the specified events shall happen the Trustees shall permit the residing party to continue to reside in the dwelling until such time as the residing party shall have signified to the Trustees in writing the wish no longer so to reside

(b) The residing party covenants with the Trustees and the personal representatives of the first of X or Y to die that he will pay all payments required under the Mortgage and that he will indemnify and keep indemnified the Trustees and the personal representatives aforesaid against all cost liabilities and claims in respect of the Mortgage

6(a) As often as the residing party shall so request in writing the Trustees may at their discretion sell the dwelling currently held by them upon the trusts of the preceding clauses and with the net proceeds of sale purchase any dwelling designated by the residing party (but if such dwelling be leasehold only if the residue of the term of years granted by the lease exceeds 60 years at the date of such designation) the total cost of which (including all legal and surveyors fees other costs fees and disbursements and stamp duty and HM Land Registry fees if appropriate) does not exceed those proceeds

(b) The Trustees shall be entitled to purchase any dwelling as aforesaid at a price in excess of such proceeds if such excess shall be provided by the residing party in which case such proportion of the future sale proceeds as such excess shall bear to the cost of purchase shall belong to the residing party absolutely on any such future sale but in the event that the future sale proceeds of the dwelling shall be less than the cost of purchase then the excess shall be reduced pro rata to the total reduction in value of the dwelling as compared with the cost of purchase

(c) if at the time of the purchase of any dwelling there should remain any surplus money in the hands of the Trustees they shall hold such surplus money upon the trusts of Clause 8 below

7 The residing party hereby covenants with the Trustees that for as long as he shall continue to reside in the dwelling he will pay the rent (if any) and other outgoings and keep the dwelling in good repair and insured comprehensively to its full value in an insurance office approved by the Trustees and in the joint names of the residing party and the Trustees and he shall within seven days of any demand being made produce to the Trustees or one of them such policy of insurance and the last receipt for premium in respect thereof and will comply with all the terms and conditions affecting the dwelling as if the residing party was the absolute owner thereof and was bound thereby and the residing party further covenants to indemnify the Trustees and each of them and their respective estates and effects against any loss damage liability charge or expense caused by or arising out of the failure by him to observe any of those terms and conditions

8 Upon the happening of any one of the specified events the Trustees shall sell the dwelling and shall stand possessed of the net proceeds of sale subject to the provisions of Clause 6

(a) as to (<u>X's contribution</u>) % for X or his personal representa-
      (total)   tives absolutely

(b) as to (<u>Y's contribution</u>) % for Y or his personal representa-
      (total)   tives absolutely

and until such sale shall take place the residing party if remaining in occupation shall remain liable to pay the outgoings referred to in clause 7 hereof and keep the dwelling in good repair and insured as required by this Declaration

9 The Trustees and each of them shall be entitled to be indemnified out of the proceeds of sale of the dwelling against all costs expenses damages claims and demands incurred or sustained by them by reason of their holding the dwelling upon the trusts hereof and in furtherance of such indemnity the Trustees shall be deemed to have all the powers (including the power of sale) given to a mortgagee under the Law of Property Act 1925 and shall be entitled to exercise the same to indemnify themselves or either of them under the provisions of this clause

10(a) If after written demand made by the Trustees in that behalf the residing party shall have failed within a period of six weeks from the date thereof to put the dwelling in good repair or to insure the same as aforesaid the Trustees may in their entire discretion effect or cause to be effected such repairs as are necessary to put the dwelling into good repair or effect such policy of insurance and the Trustees and each of them shall be entitled to an indemnity in respect of any costs or changes incurred by them in so doing and in furtherance of such indemnity the Trustees shall be deemed to have the like powers to those set out in the preceding clause hereof PROVIDED ALWAYS that the Trustees shall not be liable to see to any such insurance or repair and shall be under no liability in that respect
(b) The Trustees may borrow money using the dwelling as security if required on such terms as to interest and repayment and otherwise as they may think fit for the purpose of carrying out such repairs as required by this Declaration

11 The power of appointing a trustee in substitution for [X] shall be vested in [X] during his lifetime and after his death in his personal representatives and the power of appointing a trustee in substitution for [Y] shall be vested in [Y] during her lifetime and after her death in her personal representatives

[12 Charging clause if professional trustees:

Any trustee hereof engaged in a profession or business shall be entitled to be paid all usual professional or other charges for business transacted and acts done by him or by a partner of his in connection with the trusts hereof (whether or not in the course of his profession or business) including acts which a trustee not being in a profession or business could have done personally]

IN WITNESS etc

SCHEDULE

[see Precedent 1]
Attestation—[as Precedent 1]

Note—[as Precedent 9]

3

Property purchased by beneficial joint tenants Subsequent adjustment of interests

1 Introduction

In the majority of cases, property purchased by a husband and **3–001**
wife is purchased by them as beneficial joint tenants so that in the
event of the death of one of them, the whole property passes to
the survivor by operation of law. Such a situation is not of course
merely limited to husband and wife.

Following a change in circumstances, or a reappraisal of
circumstances it may be considered appropriate to sever the joint
tenancy so that the parties' interests are defined. Ch.2 mentioned
reasons why a property might be held as tenants in common. A
notice of severance may be served as a precautionary measure
where a co-owner wishes to dispose of his property by will and
doubt exists as to whether it is held under a joint tenancy
Carr-Glynn v Frearsons [1998] 4 All E.R. 225.

Alternatively there are circumstances where it is appropriate
that property held by tenants in common should subsequently be
held by them as beneficial joint tenants (see Precedent 16), for
instance, where cohabitees, instead of preserving their separate
interests, wish to ensure that the property passes to the survivor of
them on death outside the terms of any will or operation of the
rules of intestacy.

2 Severance

The procedure for severance differs depending upon whether title **3–002**
to the property is registered or not.

(a) Unregistered land

Section 36(2) of the Law of Property Act 1925 as amended by Trusts of Land and Appointment of Trustees Act 1996, Sch.2, para.4(1),(3), provides for severance of a joint tenancy either by:

(1) a notice in writing given by one joint tenant to the other; or

(2) the doing of such other acts or things as would, in the case of personal estate, have been effectual to sever the tenancy in equity.

Service of a notice of severance (see Precedent 11) is effective to sever the joint tenancy if properly addressed to the other joint tenant and received at the property concerned.

It would appear not to matter that the party to whom the notice is addressed does not acknowledge receipt nor that the party addressed never actually receives the notice itself (see *Re 88 Berkeley Road, London NW9; Rickwood v Turnsek* [1971] Ch. 648). This is so even if the notice is deliberately destroyed after receipt at the property by the party serving the notice because she has had a change of heart (*Kinch v Bullard* 1999 1 W.L.R. 423). See generally as to methods of severance, (1976) Conveyancer NS, col 40, p.77).

The mere issue of matrimonial proceedings for a property adjustment order does not automatically sever a joint tenancy (*Harris v Goddard* [1983] 1 W.L.R. 203) but an application in matrimonial proceedings for an order that the house should be sold and the proceeds divided equally can cause severance to occur (Re Draper's Conveyance [1969] 1 Ch. 486). The bankruptcy of one of the parties will sever the joint tenancy (Re Gorman (a bankrupt) [1990] 1 WLR 616), severance taking place at the time of the bankruptcy and not on the vesting of the property in the trustee in bankruptcy.

If a beneficial joint tenant assigns his interest this is sufficient to sever the joint tenancy as is the fraudulent dealing with the property by one joint tenant (*Ahmed v Kendrick* 1988 2 FLR 22). Severance must take place during the joint tenant's lifetime and a joint tenancy cannot be severed by will.

3–003 The joint tenants may agree that the joint tenancy should be severed, but if so they should properly evidence that fact. In *Nielson-Jones v Fedden* [1975] Ch. 222 it was held that it was not sufficient for the husband and wife to sign a memorandum to the effect that the husband was to have a free hand to sell the property and use the money to buy a new house for himself although in *Burgess v Rawnsley* [1975] Ch. 429 it was held that a beneficial joint tenancy was severed by the oral agreement of one joint tenant to sell her share in the property to the other, even though that agreement was not specifically enforceable. Similarly, drafting an agreement in the course of matrimonial negotiations can be indicative of an agreement to sever even if the agreement is not executed (*Hunter v Babbage* [1994] EGCS 8) although the actual facts would be looked at very carefully.

Whilst the joint tenancy may have been effectively severed by one of the above methods, to prevent a conveyance by the survivor, either through ignorance or fraud, it is prudent to endorse a memorandum on the last conveyance to the effect that severance has taken place. This should be sufficient to put a purchaser on notice so that he insists on paying the purchase monies to two trustees or a trust corporation so as to obtain a good receipt (Law of Property Act 1925, s.27(2) as amended by Trusts of Land and Appointment of Trustees Act 1996, s.25(1), Sch.3, para.4(1),(8)(b).

Under the Law of Property (Joint Tenants) Act 1964 a con- **3–004** veyance by the survivor of joint tenants as "beneficial owner" was sufficient to entitle any purchaser to presume that the survivor was no longer a trustee. The Law of Property (Miscellaneous Provisions) Act 1994 which came into force on July 1, 1995 requires any conveyance/transfer to contain a statement that such survivor is solely and beneficially interested in the property.

Provided such statement is given, a purchaser from a surviving joint tenant would get good title in the absence of any memorandum on the last conveyance or the registration of a bankruptcy order or a petition for such order at HM Land Charges Registry.

(b) Registered land

Section 78 of the Land Registration Act 2002 provides that, as far **3–005** as possible, reference to trusts shall be excluded from the register. A notice of severance or declaration of trust whilst being effective in equity, would have no effect on the register unless it was completed by an application to register a restriction so that the register shows that the survivor of the former two joint tenants is no longer able to give a valid receipt for capital monies.

Under the Land Registration Act 2002, s.40 and Land Registration Rules 2003, r.94(1)(b) an application for a restriction in Form A must be made using Form RX1, no fee being payable. The application may be made by or with the consent of both joint tenants (see Precedent 13)or by one proprietor without the other's consent (see Precedent 13A). In the latter case a certified copy of the receipted notice of severance or certificate that notice to sever was given in accordance with The Law of Property Act, s.36(2) must accompany the application.

The wording of the Form A restriction as set out in Sch.4 of the 2003 Rules is as follows,

"No disposition by a sole proprietor of the registered estate (except a trust corporation) under which capital money arises is to be registered unless authorised by an order of the court"

3–006 It will be appreciated that the registration of a restriction does not specify the shares in which the net proceeds of sale of the property are to be held so there should be a declaration of trust specifying those shares. Registration of a restriction does at least provide some protection and room for manoeuvre in the event of the death of a former joint tenant whilst such a declaration is being finalised.

3 THE SHARES OF THE FORMER JOINT TENANTS FOLLOWING SEVERANCE

3–007 Where no shares are agreed, severance will operate to create a tenancy in common in equal shares if the original conveyance contained an express declaration that the parties were to hold as joint tenants, *Goodman v Gallant* [1986] 1 All E.R. 311. There appears to be no direct authority on the position where there is no express declaration. It is obviously the sensible course for the shares to be agreed and specified either in the notice of severance or in a declaration of trust.

4 CONTENTS OF THE DECLARATION

3–008 These have been mentioned in Ch.2 (see pp.13–15). Where there is a "friendly" severance, the parties may decide merely to evidence that fact and set out the agreed shares (see Precedent

14), but the declaration can be extended to cover responsibility for the mortgage (see Precedent 15) and obligations as to insurance and repair (see Precedents 18 and 20).

5 RESTRICTIONS ON THE APPOINTMENT OF NEW TRUSTEES

Following severance, on the death of a trustee if there is to be a **3–009** sale a new trustee will need to be appointed of the conveyance (in unregistered land) so that a purchaser receives a good receipt for capital monies (LPA 1925, s.27(2) as amended) or for the purposes of complying with the terms of the normal joint proprietorship restriction in the case of registered land (see above, p.51–52).

In general, where there is a non-confrontational severance of a joint tenancy, the parties will probably be content that the survivor of them has power to appoint a new trustee under the provisions of the Trustee Act 1925, s.36 (see Precedents 3A and 3B).

However, this may not be considered satisfactory where there has for instance been a matrimonial dispute or where there is distrust such as in the case of a second marriage.

Whilst limitations on the appointment can be contained in the declaration of trust, it is only in registered land that these are actually brought onto the legal title by way of a restriction to that effect. The following may be considered:

(a) a replacement trustee on the death of X to be appointed by his personal representatives. This inevitably involves some little delay whilst a grant of representation to X's estate is obtained; or

(b) the appointment of a replacement trustee on the death of X to require the consent of X's personal representatives.

If either course is taken the parties should in the case of registered land apply to register a voluntary restriction in form Q using Form RX1 (see Precedent 6A).

6 STEPS TO BE TAKEN

(a) Stamp Duty Land Tax

The declarations of trust do not attract SDLT and do not require **3–010** a self certificate as they do not effect a transfer.

(b) Copies

It is prudent that each tenant in common has a copy of the declaration of trust to prove his entitlement.

(c) HM Land Registry

3–011 Application to register a form A restriction being obligatory (see above) no fee is payable. A fee of £40 per title is payable in the case of an application for any other standard form restriction, for example a form Q restriction where the consent of a deceased proprietor's personal representative is required for the appointment of a replacement trustee.

(d) Will

Where severance takes place it is appropriate that the former joint tenants review their respective wills to deal with their separate interest in the property.

Precedent 11—Notice of Severance by one joint tenant to the other severing joint tenancy. Unregistered land.

To [*full name and address of other joint tenant*]

I HEREBY GIVE YOU NOTICE severing our joint tenancy in **3–011** equity of and in the Property details of which are given in the Schedule hereto now held by yourself and myself as joint tenants both at law and in equity and henceforth the Property shall be held by us as tenants in common in:

— equal shares (or whatever shares are agreed) or

— upon the terms of a Declaration of Trust signed by us

I REQUEST that you acknowledge receipt of this notice by signing and returning the Duplicate Notice enclosed.

SCHEDULE

[*description of Property*]

Date
Signed [signature of joint tenant giving notice]

Duplicate
I acknowledge receipt of this Notice of Severance of which the above is a duplicate
Date
Signed [signature of recipient]

Precedent 12—Unregistered land. Memorandum of Severance to be endorsed on last conveyance.

Memorandum

3–012 By a Notice of Severance dated   addressed by
the within named [X] to the within named [Y] the beneficial joint
tenancy herein created was severed.

Precedent 13—Registered land. Application by both proprieter to enter a form A Restriction under LRR 2003 R94(1)(b) on severance

Application to enter a restriction	Land Registry	RX1

If you need more room than is provided for in a panel, use continuation sheet CS and attach to this form.

1. Administrative area and postcode if known   [AREA]

2. Title number(s) [TITLE NUMBER]

3. If you have already made this application by **outline application,** insert reference number:

4. Property *Insert address or other description.*
[ADDRESS]

The restriction applied for is to affect *Place "X" in the appropriate box and complete as necessary.*

☒ the whole of each registered estate

☐ the part(s) of the registered estate(s) shown on the attached plan by *State reference e.g. "edged red".*

☐ the registered charge(s) dated   in favour of   referred to in the Charges Register

5. Application and fee *A fee calculator for all types of applications can be found on Land Registry's website at www.landregistry.gov.uk/fees*

Restriction   Fee paid £

Fee payment method: *Place "X" in the appropriate box.*

I wish to pay the appropriate fee payable under the current Land Registration Fee Order:

☐ by cheque or postal order, amount £_____ made payable to "Land Registry".

☐ by Direct Debit under an authorised agreement with Land Registry.

FOR OFFICIAL USE ONLY
Record of fee paid

Particulars of under/over payment

Fees debited £

Reference number

6. Documents lodged with this application *If this application is accompanied by either Form AP1 or FR1 please only complete the corresponding panel on Form AP1 or DL. Number the documents in sequence; copies should also be numbered and listed as separate documents, alternatively you may prefer to use Form DL. If you supply the original document and a certified copy, we shall assume that you request the return of the original; if a certified copy is not supplied, we may retain the original document and it may be destroyed.*

7. The applicant is: *Please provide the full name of the person applying for the restriction.*
[X] AND [Y]

The application has been lodged by:
Land Registry Key No. (if appropriate)
Name (if different from the applicant)
Address/DX No.   [ADDRESS]

Reference
E-mail

Telephone No.	Fax No.

FOR OFFICIAL USE ONLY
Codes
Dealing

Status

8. Where you would like us to deal with someone else *We shall deal only with the applicant, or the person lodging the application if different, unless you place "X" against one or more of the statements below and give the necessary details.*

☐ Send title information document to the person shown below

☐ Raise any requisitions or queries with the person shown below

☐ Return original documents lodged with this form (see note in panel 6) to the person shown below
If this applies only to certain documents, please specify.

Name
Address/DX No.

Reference
E-mail

Telephone No.	Fax No.

9. Entitlement to apply for a restriction *Place "X" in the appropriate box.*

☒ The applicant is the registered proprietor of the registered estate/charge referred to in panel 4.

☐ The applicant is the person **entitled** to be registered as proprietor of the registered estate/charge referred to in panel 4. **Complete panel 12.**

☐ The consent of the registered proprietor of the registered estate/charge referred to in panel 4 accompanies this application or the applicant's conveyancer certifies that he holds this consent. **Complete panel 11.**

☐ The consent of the person **entitled** to be registered as proprietor of the registered estate/charge referred to in panel 4 accompanies this application or the applicant's conveyancer certifies that he holds this consent. **Complete panels 11 and 12.**

☐ Evidence that the applicant has sufficient interest in the making of the entry of the restriction applied for in panel 10 accompanies this application. **Complete panel 13.**

10. The applicant applies to enter the following restriction against the registered estate/charge referred to in panel 4: *Please set out the form of restriction required. Schedule 4 to the Land Registration Rules 2003 contains standard forms of restrictions. Use this form to apply for a standard form of restriction (as set out in Schedule 4 to the Land Registration Rules 2003) or, where appropriate, a restriction in another form. If the restriction is not a standard form of restriction, the registrar must be satisfied that the terms of the proposed restriction are reasonable and that applying the proposed restriction would be straightforward and not place an unreasonable burden on him. If the restriction requires notice to be given to a person, requires a person's consent or certificate or is a standard form restriction that refers to a named person, include that person's address for service.*

No disposition by a sole proprietor of the registered estate (except a trust corporation) under which capital money arises is to be registered unless authorised by an order of the court.

11. Evidence of consent *Please complete this panel if instructed to do so in panel 9. Place "X" in the appropriate box.*

☐ The [registered proprietor of][person entitled to be registered as the proprietor of] the registered estate/charge referred to in panel 4 consents to the entry of the restriction and that person or their conveyancer has completed panel 15.

☐ I am the applicant's conveyancer and certify that I hold the consent referred to in panel 9.

☐ The consent referred to in panel 9 is contained on page _____ of the document numbered _____ referred to in [panel 6][Form AP1][Form DL].

12. Evidence of entitlement to be registered as proprietor *Please complete this panel if instructed to do so in panel 9. Place "X" in the appropriate box.*

☐ I am the applicant's conveyancer and certify that I am satisfied that the applicant/person consenting to this application is entitled to be registered as proprietor and that I hold the originals of the documents that contain evidence of that person's entitlement, or an application for registration of that person as proprietor is pending at Land Registry.

☐ Evidence that the applicant/person consenting to this application is entitled to be registered as proprietor is contained in the document(s) numbered _____ referred to in [panel 6][Form AP1][Form DL].

13. Evidence that the applicant has sufficient interest *Please complete this panel if instructed to do so in panel 9.*

State brief details of the applicant's interest in the making of the entry of the restriction applied for in panel 10.

Evidence of this interest is contained in the document(s) numbered referred to in [panel 6] [Form AP1][Form DL].

14. Signature of applicant

or their conveyancer _____ **Date** _____

15. Consent
Consent to the entry of the restriction specified in panel 10 is given by:

Names BLOCK LETTERS	**Signatures**
1.	1.
2.	2.
3.	3.

Precedent 13A—Registered land. Application by one joint tenant following service a notice of severance without the consent of the other under s.43(1)(c) LRA 2002.

Application to enter
a restriction

Land Registry

RX1

If you need more room than is provided for in a panel, use continuation sheet CS and attach to this form.

1. Administrative area and postcode if known   [AREA]
2. Title number(s) [TITLE NUMBER]

3. If you have already made this application by **outline application,** insert reference number:

4. Property *Insert address or other description.*
[ADDRESS]
The restriction applied for is to affect *Place "X" in the appropriate box and complete as necessary.*

☐ the whole of each registered estate

☐ the part(s) of the registered estate(s) shown on the attached plan by *State reference e.g. "edged red".*

☐ the registered charge(s) dated   in favour of
        referred to in the Charges Register

5. Application and fee *A fee calculator for all types of applications can be found on Land Registry's website at www.landregistry.gov.uk/fees*	FOR OFFICIAL USE ONLY Record of fee paid
Restriction Fee paid £	
Fee payment method: *Place "X" in the appropriate box.*	Particulars of under/over payment
I wish to pay the appropriate fee payable under the current Land Registration Fee Order:	
☐ by cheque or postal order, amount £_____ made payable to "Land Registry".	Fees debited £
☐ by Direct Debit under an authorised agreement with Land Registry.	Reference number

6. Documents lodged with this application *If this application is accompanied by either Form AP1 or FR1 please only complete the corresponding panel on Form AP1 or DL. Number the documents in sequence; copies should also be numbered and listed as separate documents, alternatively you may prefer to use Form DL. If you supply the original document and a certified copy, we shall assume that you request the return of the original; if a certified copy is not supplied, we may retain the original document and it may be destroyed.*

[Certified copy of notice of severance (signed by other joint tenant to acknowledge receipt) or Certificate signed by applicant or their conveyancer that notice to sever was given in accordance with s.36(2) Law of Property Act 1925]

7. The applicant is: *Please provide the full name of the person applying for the restriction.* [X] (JOINT TENANT SERVING NOTICE OF SEVERANCE)	
The application has been lodged by: Land Registry Key No. (if appropriate) Name (if different from the applicant) Address/DX No. [ADDRESS] Reference E-mail	FOR OFFICIAL USE ONLY Codes Dealing Status
Telephone No. Fax No.	

8. Where you would like us to deal with someone else *We shall deal only with the applicant, or the person lodging the application if different, unless you place "X" against one or more of the statements below and give the necessary details.*

☐ Send title information document to the person shown below

☐ Raise any requisitions or queries with the person shown below

☐ Return original documents lodged with this form (see note in panel 6) to the person shown below
   If this applies only to certain documents, please specify.

Name
Address/DX No.

Reference
E-mail

Telephone No.	Fax No.

9. Entitlement to apply for a restriction *Place "X" in the appropriate box.*

☐ The applicant is the registered proprietor of the registered estate/charge referred to in panel 4.

☐ The applicant is the person **entitled** to be registered as proprietor of the registered estate/charge referred to in panel 4. **Complete panel 12.**

☐ The consent of the registered proprietor of the registered estate/charge referred to in panel 4 accompanies this application or the applicant's conveyancer certifies that he holds this consent. **Complete panel 11.**

☐ The consent of the person **entitled** to be registered as proprietor of the registered estate/charge referred to in panel 4 accompanies this application or the applicant's conveyancer certifies that he holds this consent. **Complete panels 11 and 12.**

☒ Evidence that the applicant has sufficient interest in the making of the entry of the restriction applied for in panel 10 accompanies this application. **Complete panel 13.**

10. The applicant applies to enter the following restriction against the registered estate/charge referred to in panel 4: *Please set out the form of restriction required. Schedule 4 to the Land Registration Rules 2003 contains standard forms of restrictions. Use this form to apply for a standard form of restriction (as set out in Schedule 4 to the Land Registration Rules 2003) or, where appropriate, a restriction in another form. If the restriction is not a standard form of restriction, the registrar must be satisfied that the terms of the proposed restriction are reasonable and that applying the proposed restriction would be straightforward and not place an unreasonable burden on him. If the restriction requires notice to be given to a person, requires a person's consent or certificate or is a standard form restriction that refers to a named person, include that person's address for service.*

No disposition by a sole proprieter of the registered estate (except a trust corporation) under which capital money arises is to be registered unless authorised by an order of the court.

11. Evidence of consent *Please complete this panel if instructed to do so in panel 9. Place "X" in the appropriate box.*

☐ The [registered proprietor of][person entitled to be registered as the proprietor of] the registered estate/charge referred to in panel 4 consents to the entry of the restriction and that person or their conveyancer has completed panel 15.

☐ I am the applicant's conveyancer and certify that I hold the consent referred to in panel 9.

☐ The consent referred to in panel 9 is contained on page ____ of the document numbered ____ referred to in [panel 6][Form AP1][Form DL].

12. Evidence of entitlement to be registered as proprietor *Please complete this panel if instructed to do so in panel 9. Place "X" in the appropriate box.*

☐ I am the applicant's conveyancer and certify that I am satisfied that the applicant/person consenting to this application is entitled to be registered as proprietor and that I hold the originals of the documents that contain evidence of that person's entitlement, or an application for registration of that person as proprietor is pending at Land Registry.

☐ Evidence that the applicant/person consenting to this application is entitled to be registered as proprietor is contained in the document(s) numbered ____ referred to in [panel 6][Form AP1][Form DL].

13. Evidence that the applicant has sufficient interest *Please complete this panel if instructed to do so in panel 9.*

State brief details of the applicant's interest in the making of the entry of the restriction applied for in panel 10.

The applicant and [Y] (other joint tenant) are the registered proprieters of the registered estate. The applicant severed the the beneficial joint tenancy by notice of severance given to Y dated [   ]

Evidence of this interest is contained in the document(s) numbered referred to in [panel 6] [Form AP1][Form DL].

14. Signature of applicant

or their conveyancer _____ **Date** _____

15. Consent
Consent to the entry of the restriction specified in panel 10 is given by:

Names BLOCK LETTERS	Signatures
1.	1.
2.	2.
3.	3.

Precedent 14—Property held by beneficial joint tenants, severance, property henceforth to be held in defined shares. No mortgage.

THIS DECLARATION OF TRUST is made this   day of **3–014**
           200
BETWEEN   (1)   [X]   of   [*address*]   and   (2)   [Y]
of   [*address*]

WHEREAS:

(A) By a Conveyance/Transfer dated   the property ("the Property") details of which are contained in the Schedule hereto was conveyed/transferred to [X] and [Y] to be held by them [*unregistered land*] as beneficial joint tenants
or [*registered land*] on the basis that the survivor of them could give a good receipt for capital monies being beneficial joint tenants.

(B) The parties have agreed that their joint tenancy of the Property should be severed and that henceforth their interests in the Property and its proceeds of sale and net rents and profits thereof until sale shall be held as hereinafter mentioned.

NOW THIS DEED WITNESSES as follows:

1 The parties hereto DECLARE that with effect from the date hereof they hold the Property on a trust of land

2 The parties hereto DECLARE that with effect from the date hereof they hold the Property and its proceeds of sale (after deducting therefrom the costs of sale) and the net rents and profits until sale UPON TRUST for themselves as tenants in common

(a) as to [60%] for X absolutely

(b) as to [40%] for Y absolutely

3 [*registered land*] The parties hereto COVENANT with each other to sign such application as may be necessary to enter the appropriate restriction at HM Land Registry to give effect to this Deed

IN WITNESS etc

SCHEDULE

[*see Precedent 1*]

Attestation—[*as Precedent 1*]

Note:

- (a) unregistered title—put Memorandum on last Conveyance (see Precedent 12)
- (b) registered title—apply to HMLR on Form RX1 (see Precedent 13)

Precedent 15—Property held by beneficial joint tenants subject to mortgage. Severance and agreement to hold and pay mortgage in defined shares.

THIS DECLARATION OF TRUST is made this   day of **3–015**
        200

BETWEEN   (1)   [X]   of   [*address*]
and   (2)   [Y]   of   [*address*]

WHEREAS:

(A) [*As Precedent 14 recital (A)*]

(B) By a Mortgage ("the Mortgage") dated   and made between (1) the parties hereto and (2) [*Building Society*] the Property was charged to the said Society to secure the sum of £

(C) The parties have agreed that their joint tenancy should be severed and that henceforth their interests in the Property and its proceeds of sale and net rents and profits thereof until sale shall be held as hereinafter mentioned subject to the Mortgage

NOW THIS DEED WITNESSES as follows:

1 The parties hereto DECLARE that with effect from the date hereof they hold the Property on a trust of land

2. The parties hereto DECLARE that with effect from the date hereof they hold the Property and the proceeds of sale (after discharging the mortgage and deducting therefrom the costs of sale) and the net rents and profits until sale UPON TRUST for themselves as tenants in common

   (a) as to [60%] for X absolutely

   (b) as to [40%] for Y absolutely

and upon the basis that the Mortgage shall be repaid as to 60% by [X] and as to 40% by [Y]

3 The parties hereto COVENANT with each other to pay the payments due under the Mortgage in the same percentage as their entitlement as set out in Clause 1 and to indemnify the other and his estate and effects against all costs claims and demands in respect of the Mortgage to the limit of the percentage before mentioned

4 [*registered land*] [As Precedent 14 clause 3]

   IN WITNESS etc

SCHEDULE
[*see Precedent 1*]

Attestation—[*as Precedent 1*]

Note:—as Precedent 14

Precedent 16—Property held as tenants in common in equal shares now to be held by them as beneficial joint tenants.

THIS DECLARATION OF TRUST is made this   day of **3–016**
          200
BETWEEN   (1)   [X]   of   [address]   and   (2)   [Y]
of   [address]

WHEREAS:

(A) The property ("the Property") details of which are contained in the Schedule hereto
[unregistered land] is presently held by the parties hereto as trustees for themselves as tenants in common in equal shares
or [registered land] is registered in the names of the parties hereto subject to the restriction that the survivor of them is unable to give a valid receipt for capital monies

(B) The parties have agreed that henceforth they should hold the Property as beneficial joint tenants

NOW THIS DEED WITNESSES as follows:

1 The parties hereto DECLARE that with effect from the date hereof they shall hold the Property on a trust of land and hold the same and the net proceeds of sale and the net income until sale UPON TRUST for themselves as beneficial joint tenants

2 [registered land] The parties hereto COVENANT to apply to HM Land Registry to cancel the restriction recited above and to amend the register to the effect that the survivor of them can give a valid receipt for capital money arising on a disposition of the land comprised in the title below mentioned

   IN WITNESS etc

SCHEDULE
[see Precedent 1]

Attestation—[as Precedent 1]

Precedent 17—Registered land. Application to cancel restriction to give effect to precedent 16 (Form RX3)

Application to cancel a restriction	**Land Registry** **RX3**

3–017 *To apply for an order to disapply/modify a restriction, use Form RX2. To apply to withdraw a restriction, use Form RX4.*
If you need more room than is provided for in a panel, use continuation sheet CS and attach to this form.

---

1. Administrative area and postcode if known.
    [AREA]

2. Title number(s)
    [TITLE NUMBER]

3. If you have already made this application by **outline application,** insert the reference number:

4. Property
    [ADDRESS]

5. Documents lodged with this form *If this application is accompanied by Form AP1, please only complete the corresponding panel on that form. Number the documents in sequence; copies should also be numbered and listed as separate documents. If you supply the original document and a certified copy, we shall assume that you request the return of the original; if a certified copy is not supplied, we may retain the original document and it may be destroyed.*

Declaration of trust dated [   ] made between [X] and [Y] and certified copy of the same

6. The applicant is: *Please provide the full name of the person applying for the cancellation of the restriction.*

The application has been lodged by:
Land Registry Key No. (if appropriate)
Name (if different from the applicant)
Address/DX No.   [ADDRESS]

Reference
E-mail

FOR OFFICIAL USE ONLY
Codes
Dealing
Status

Telephone No. | Fax No.

7. Application: *Place "X" in the appropriate box and complete as necessary.*

The applicant applies to cancel the restriction registered against the title number(s) listed in panel 2 which relate(s) to: *If more than one restriction relates to the registered estate/charge, give further details to identify which is to be cancelled.*

☒ the registered estate

☐ that part of the registered estate shown on the attached plan by *State reference e.g. "edged red".*

☐ the registered charge dated   in favour of
    referred to in the Charges Register

8. State why the restriction is no longer required:
The applicants have become entitled as beneficial joint tenants by virtue of a declaration of trust dated [   ]

9. Signature of applicant or their conveyancer _____ Date _____

Crown copyright (ref: LR/HQ/CD-ROM) 6/03

Precedent 18—Matrimonial home originally held by husband and wife as beneficial joint tenants. Tenancy now severed and house to be held upon terms of Court Order. Unregistered and registered land. No mortgage.

THIS DECLARATION OF TRUST is made the   day of **3–018**
           200

BY [*Husband*] of   [*address*] ["the Husband"] and [*Wife*] of   [*address*] ("the Wife")

WHEREAS:

unregistered land

(A) By a conveyance ("the Conveyance") dated   and made between (1)   and (2)   the Husband and the Wife the Property details of which are contained in the Schedule hereto was conveyed to the Husband and the Wife in fee simple as beneficial joint tenants

(B) Following an Order of [Deputy] District Judge
in the County Court dated   in proceedings between the parties hereto bearing number   the joint tenancy created by the Conveyance was severed as the parties hereto hereby admit and it was ordered that the Property be held upon the terms hereinafter mentioned

registered land

(A) The Husband and the Wife are registered as the proprietors at HM Land Registry of the Property details of which are contained in the Schedule hereto

(B) Following an Order of [Deputy] District Judge
in the County Court dated   and in proceedings between the Husband and the Wife bearing number   it was ordered that the Property be held upon the terms hereinafter mentioned and the Husband and Wife have also applied to HM Land Registry to enter a restriction to the effect that except under an order of the Registrar no disposition is to be registered after the death of either of them without the consent of the personal representatives of the deceased

NOW IT IS HEREBY DECLARED as follows:

1 In pursuance of the Court Order from *the date thereof* the parties shall hold the Property as trustees of land upon the terms of the Court Order

2. In pursuance of the Court Order and from the date thereof the parties shall hold the Property and its net proceeds of sale (after deducting therefrom the costs of sale) and the net rents and profits until sale in trust for themselves as tenants in common

  (a) as to [60%] for the Husband absolutely

  (b) as to [40%] for the Wife absolutely and otherwise upon the terms of the Court Order.

3 The Wife covenants with the Husband that she will keep the Property in good repair and insured comprehensively to its full value in an insurance office approved by the Husband and in the joint names of herself and the Husband and she shall within seven days of any demand being made produce to the Husband such policy of insurance and the last receipt for premium in respect thereof

  IN WITNESS etc

SCHEDULE

[brief description of property from title documents]

Attestation—*[as Precedent 1]*

Note:

  (a) unregistered title—put memorandum on last conveyance (see Precedent 12)

  (b) register title—apply to HMLR on form RX1 (see Precedents 6A and 13)

Precedent 19—Matrimonial home originally held by husband and wife as beneficial joint tenants. Tenancy now severed and house held upon terms of Court Order. Mortgage—husband to be responsible until sale.

THIS DECLARATION OF TRUST is made the   day **3–019** of   200

BY [*Husband*] of   [*address*] ("the Husband") and [*Wife*] of   [*address*] ("the Wife")

WHEREAS:

(A) [*Precedent 18 Recital* (A) as appropriate]

(B) By a Mortgage ("the Mortgage") dated   and made between (1) the Husband and the Wife and (2) the Building Society ("the Society") the Property was charged to the Society to secure the sum of £

(C) The sum of £   is now owing to the Society on the security of the Mortgage

(D) [Precedent 18 recital (B) as appropriate continue "with the Husband being solely responsible for the monies due under the Mortgage."

NOW IT IS HEREBY DECLARED:

1 In pursuance of the Court Order and as from the date thereof the Husband and the Wife shall hold the Property as trustees of land upon the terms of the Court Order.

2. In pursuance of the Court Order and from the date thereof the parties shall hold the Property and the net proceeds of sale (which for the avoidance of doubt shall mean the sum remaining after discharge of the mortgage and payment of all the costs of sale) and the net rents and profits until sale UPON TRUST for themselves as tenants in common.

   (a) as to [60%] for the Husband absolutely

   (b) as to [40%] for the Wife absolutely

and otherwise upon the terms of the Court Order.

3 The Husband covenants with the Wife that with effect from [*usually a date specified in the Court Order*] and until the Property

be sold he will pay and discharge all principal monies interest costs and other monies secured by or henceforth to become payable under the Mortgage and will at all times indemnify and keep indemnified the Wife and her estate and effects against all proceedings costs claims and demands in respect thereof

4 [covenant to repair—see Precedent 18, clause 3]

IN WITNESS etc

SCHEDULE

[*brief description of property from title documents*]

Attestation—[*as Precedent 1*]

Note: as Precedent 18

Precedent 20—Dwelling-house held by trustees upon trust until the happening of certain events and then for former husband and wife in unequal shares, occupying wife to be responsible for repairs etc. Power to change the property for another. Registered land.

THIS DECLARATION OF TRUST is made the   day of **3–020**
     200

By   (1)   [X]   of   [address]   and   [Y] of   [address] together called "the Trustees" which expression shall include all other the trustee or trustees for the time being hereof) and (2) [Wife] of   ("the Wife")

WHEREAS:

(A) By a Transfer bearing the same date as but executed before this Declaration and made between (1) [Husband] and [Wife] and (2) the Trustees the property briefly described in the Schedule hereto ("the Property") was transferred to the Trustees

(B) The Trustees make this Declaration to set out the trusts and the powers and provisions subject to which the Property is held

NOW IT IS HEREBY DECLARED as follows:

1 The following expressions shall have the following meanings:
(a) "the dwelling" shall mean ALL THAT the Property and any house bungalow flat or maisonette purchased by the Trustees in accordance with the provisions hereof in substitution for the Property
(b) "the specified events" shall mean:

     (i) (a) the eighteenth birthday of [A—*youngest child*] who was born on   [date] or
         (b) the date upon which [A] shall cease full time education whichever is the later or

    (ii) the death of the Wife or

   (iii) the re-marriage of the Wife

whichever shall first occur
(c) "the net proceeds of sale" shall mean the proceeds of sale of the dwelling after payment of the costs of sale

2 The Trustees shall hold the dwelling as trustees of land

3 The Trustees may permit the Wife to reside in and continue to reside in the dwelling without payment therefor made by her to the Trustees and provided none of the specified events shall happen the Trustees shall permit the Wife to continue to reside in the dwelling until such time as she shall have signified to the Trustees in writing her wish no longer so to reside

4(a) As often as the Wife shall so request in writing the Trustees may at their discretion sell the dwelling currently held by them upon the trusts of the preceding clauses and with the net proceeds of sale purchase any dwelling designated by the Wife (but if such dwelling be leasehold only if the residue of the term of years granted by the lease exceeds 60 years at the date of such designation) the total cost of which (including all legal and surveyors fees other costs fees and disbursements and stamp duty and HM Land Registry fees if appropriate) does not exceed those proceeds

(b) The Trustees shall be entitled to purchase any dwelling as aforesaid at a price in excess of such proceeds if such excess shall be provided by the Wife in which case such proportion of the future sale proceeds as such excess shall bear to the cost of purchase shall belong to the Wife absolutely on any such future sale but in the event that the future sale proceeds of the dwelling shall be less than the cost of purchase then the excess shall be reduced pro rata to the total reduction in value of the dwelling as compared with the cost of purchase

(c) If at the time of the purchase of any dwelling there should remain any surplus money in the hands of the Trustees they shall hold such surplus money upon the trusts of Clause 6 below

5 The Wife hereby covenants with the Trustees that for as long as she shall continue to reside in the dwelling she will pay the rent (if any) and other outgoings and keep the dwelling in good repair and insured comprehensively to its full value in an insurance office approved by the Trustees and in the joint names of herself and the Trustees and she shall within seven days of any demand being made produce to the Trustees or one of them such policy of insurance and the last receipt for premium in respect thereof and she will comply with all the terms and conditions affecting the dwelling as if she was the absolute owner thereof and was bound thereby and the Wife further covenants to indemnify the Trustees

and each of them and their respective estates and effects against any loss damage liability charge or expense caused by or arising out of the failure by her to observe any of the terms and conditions aforesaid

6 Upon the happening of any one of the specified events the Trustees shall sell the dwelling and shall stand possessed of the net proceeds of sale subject to the provisions of Clause 4:

    (i) as to 60 per cent for [*Husband*] or his personal representatives (as the case may be)

    (ii) as to 40 per cent for the Wife or her personal representatives (as the case may be) less any monies due to the Trustees by reason of the indemnities herein contained

and until such sale shall take place the Wife if remaining in occupation shall remain liable to pay the outgoings referred to in clause 5 hereof and keep the dwelling in good repair and insured as required by this Declaration

7 The Trustees and each of them shall be entitled to be indemnified out of the proceeds of sale of the dwelling against all costs expenses damages claims and demands incurred or sustained by them by reason of their holding the dwelling upon the trusts hereof and in furtherance of such indemnity the Trustees shall be deemed to have all the powers (including the power of sale) given to a mortgagee under the Law of Property Act 1925 and shall be entitled to exercise the same to indemnify themselves or either of them under the provisions of this clause

8(a) If after written demand made by the Trustees in that behalf the Wife shall have failed within a period of six weeks from the date thereof to put the dwelling in good repair or to insure the same as aforesaid the Trustees may in their entire discretion effect or cause to be effected such repairs as are necessary to put the dwelling into good repair or effect such policy of insurance and the Trustees and each of them shall be entitled to an indemnity in respect of any costs or charges incurred by them in so doing and in furtherance of such indemnity the Trustees shall be deemed to have the like powers to those set out in the preceding clause hereof PROVIDED ALWAYS that the Trustees shall not be liable to see to any such insurance or repair and shall be under no liability in that respect

(b) The Trustees may borrow money using the dwelling as security if required on such terms as to interest and repayment and otherwise as they may think fit for the purpose of carrying out such repairs as required by this Declaration

9 The power of appointing a trustee in substitution for [X] shall be vested in [Husband] during his lifetime and after his death in his personal representatives and the power of appointing a trustee in substitution for [Y] shall be vested in the Wife during her lifetime and after her death in her personal representatives

[10 *Charging clause if professional trustees:*
Any trustee hereof engaged in a profession or business shall be entitled to be paid all usual professional or other charges for business transacted and acts done by him or by a partner of his in connection with the trusts hereof (whether or not in the course of his profession or business) including acts which a trustee not being in a profession or business could have done personally]

IN WITNESS etc

SCHEDULE

[*see Precedent 1*]

Attestation—[*as Precedent 1*]

Note: Application to be made to HMLR on form RX1 for restriction to reflect powers of appointment of trustees (see precedent 6A)

4

Legal owner of dwellinghouse holding for another (or for self and another)

1. INTRODUCTION

It is not unusual for a sole homeowner to want to recognise the **4–001** equity that someone else may have contributed. Whilst this can be solved by the owner conveying/transferring the property into joint names to be held as a joint tenants or tenants in common (in which latter case a declaration of trust should be made; see Precedent 1), this may not be convenient (for examples see below) and a declaration of trust, whilst not psychologically the same, can achieve the same result in equity.

Similarly, an individual may have a personal right to buy a property but be financially unable to do so. Again, if the money is provided by someone else, the provider's interest can be recognised by the individual making a declaration of trust.

2. NOMINEE CONVEYANCE

If mere anonymity is required at the time of the purchase, then **4–002** the appropriate course is for an individual to complete the purchase and then immediately make a "nominee conveyance" to the true purchaser (see precedent in Encyclopaedia of Forms and Precedents (5th ed., Butterworths), Vol 37 p.461.

Such a situation may arise where for instance an agent completes the purchase of a property bought at auction and immediately following completion transfers the property to the party for whom he acted and who put up the purchase price.

4–003   If, however, it is intended that the property should remain in the nominee's name for the time being, then the appropriate course is for the nominee to make a declaration of trust (see Precedent 21). This can leave the real owner a little exposed should the trustee be unscrupulous, and the real owner should be advised:

(1) in the case of unregistered land to ensure that he (the real owner) holds the title documents, to consider the appointment of a further trustee (on the grounds that one person may be unscrupulous but two are less likely to be so!) and to register a caution against first registration, so that the real owner will learn about any application to HM Land Registry and have the opportunity to oppose it.

Application for registration of a caution must be made on the prescribed form CT1 (Land Registration Rules 2003 r.42) and must sufficiently identify the land, preferably by plan. It must be accompanied by a statutory declaration showing the interest the cautioner claims in the land, in this case that he is the beneficial owner, and

(2) in the case of registered land, in theory, because the land is held on trust, the registered proprietor as sole trustee is obliged to apply for the entry of a form A restriction preventing sale by a sole trustee (Land Registration Rules 2003,r.94(2)). The Registrar is not obliged to enter such restriction automatically and in practice may not be made aware that the proprietor holds as trustee. However, if the sole trustee fails to apply for this restriction the real owner may apply for its entry as a person who has an interest in the registered estate (Land Registration Act 2002, s 43(1) (c) and Land Registration Rules 2003, r.93(a),(see Precedent 28)). In the absence of the consent of the registered proprietor the Registrar will serve notice of the application on him, giving him 15 business days to object (Land Registration Act 2002, s.45, Land Registration Rules 2003, r.92(9). He may also apply for a restriction in form N preventing the registration of dispositions without the real owner's consent (Land Registration Rules 2003, Sch.4, Form N) (see Precedent 29).

3. The Council House

4–004 The Housing Act 1985 gave occupiers of houses owned by their local authority or New Town Development Corporation a right to buy the house and this right was extended to certain tenants of registered social landlords by the Housing Act 1996. Discounts on the value of the property depending upon the length of occupation can make such a purchase an attractive proposition.

The discount is only available to the occupying tenant, who is often elderly or without means to purchase. However, someone within the family may be prepared to provide the finances necessary for the purchase and it is this contributor's position that should be protected.

This can be done by:

(1) a declaration of trust being made by the legal owner (the council tenant); and

(2) registering a restriction at HM Land Registry (see above). The question of unregistered land does not arise because any such purchase is subject to compulsory registration of title (Housing Act 1985, s.154).

A relevant disposal (see Housing Act 1985, s.159) of the dwelling within three years of purchase (Housing and Planning Act 1986, s.2(3)) triggers repayment of the discount, the amount being by reference to the number of years since purchase. It is worth noting that the vesting of the whole of the dwellinghouse in a person taking under a will or on intestacy, or if the disposal is pursuant to a property adjustment order in matrimonial proceedings where continuing occupation is envisaged, are exempt disposals as are certain disposals to family members and do not trigger repayment of the discount (Housing Act 1985, s.160).

It is important that the parties (i.e. the person with the right to **4–005** buy ("the occupier") and the contributor) consider:

(1) is there to be a provision at the end of the repayment of discount period whereby the contributor can require the property to be transferred to his name? This will probably depend upon the agreed "stake" (if any) of the occupier in the property;

(2) should the position of the occupier be protected by a lease so as to give security of tenure or a provision agreed so that the property cannot be sold without his consent? This is important—the elderly council tenant could count on security of tenure. If her son provides the purchase price

and then has matrimonial proceedings, the estranged daughter-in-law might press for a sale of the former council house so as to unlock monies. Alternatively the son could become insolvent and his trustee in bankruptcy press for a sale;

(3) if the occupier is to have a stake in the property how are the respective interests to be dealt with during the "repayment of discount period", and thereafter? and

(4) who is to pay the outgoings such as insurance and cost of repairs?

4–006 Of the precedents that follow, Precedent 22 recognises the contributor's stake and after repayment of that, splits the balance (say) 50/50 between the owner and the contributor. The precedent can easily be adapted (in the Schedule) to recognise an amount that the owner may have paid by varying the percentage due to the contributor.

Precedent 23 deals with a case where a mortgage is effected and discharged by the former council tenant. It must be agreed how this is to affect the interests of the parties; as drafted the contributor benefits as the mortgage is reduced thus to an extent compensating him for money laid out on which he is getting no return.

Precedent 24 provides for the proceeds of sale (after repayment of any discount) to be split between the owner's grandchild and the contributor (i.e. the owner's grandchild gets some of the benefit of the discount at the end of the day). The precedent therefore contains additional provisions to cope with the appointment of trustees and deal with the proceeds of sale in the event that the grandchild is a minor at the relevant time—hence the additional precedent concerning an appointment of trustees (Precedent 25).

4. RECOGNITION OF ANOTHER'S CONTRIBUTION

4–007 It is not uncommon for a person to join a sole proprietor of a property and subsequently spend his or her own money improving or extending it. Particularly if the parties are not married, the party who has expended money ("the contributor") may wish to acquire a formal interest in the property.

If the property is subject to a mortgage then to place the title into the joint names of the parties will invariably require the consent of the mortgagee, and the contributor will be expected to covenant in favour of the mortgagee. Costs will be involved.

Similarly, a property may have been purchased in one name (because a spouse or partner was not available or did not want to be involved in any mortgage application) and it is necessary to recognise the contributor's share or contribution. The transfer or conveyance into joint names will incur costs and, if there is a mortgagee involved, require the mortgagee's consent and satisfaction of other conditions.

It is simpler and cheaper that the property remain in the name of the sole proprietor. The following points should also be borne in mind.

(a) Unregistered land

The proprietor should execute a declaration of trust to the effect **4–008** that the property is held in specified shares for the proprietor and the contributor. Because the declaration will not affect the legal title, a caution against first registration should also be lodged (see above, p.78).

(b) Registered land

The registered owner should execute a declaration of trust as above. A form A restriction should be entered together with a form B restriction if there are further limitations on the powers of the registered owner as sole trustee, for example, if such trustee cannot dispose without the consent of the contributor or his personal representatives. Precedents 26 and 27 can be adapted to either registered or unregistered land.

5. TRANSFER OF ENTIRE BENEFICIAL OWNERSHIP

In contrast to the earlier section where property stood in the **4–009** name of one person who wished to recognise the contribution or entitlement of another, there are cases where the sole owner wishes the entire beneficial entitlement to be transferred to another, but is unable to transfer/convey the legal estate without difficulty or expense. A typical situation would be where a husband owns a house subject to mortgage in his sole name and wishes to put it into his wife's name. This could involve a heavy liability to stamp duty land tax.

If on a transfer of property subject to a debt (and not a transfer of property in connection with divorce under Finance Act 2003, Sch.3 para.3) the transferee covenants (either in the transfer or separately) to pay the debt or indemnify the transferor in respect thereof, such a covenant constitutes chargeable consideration and establishes the transaction as a land transaction on which SDLT is payable (see Finance Act 2003 Sch.4, para.8). The position is similar to the former position under Stamp Duty as to which see Inland Revenue Statement of Practice, SP6/90 dated April 27, 1990.

Where no express covenant is given by the transferee the Revenue takes the view that one is implied unless a contrary intention is shown. Thus, unless Finance Act 2003 Sch.3, para.3 above applies, a mortgaged property transferred from one person to another will incur a charge to stamp duty unless it is clear that the transferor alone remains liable for the debt. This is unlikely if there is a transfer of the legal estate, for the mortgagee will in most cases be taking a covenant from the transferee. It is appropriate therefore that legal title and the mortgage liability remain with the transferor, the equity in effect moving across via a declaration of trust (see Precedent 30).

Of course, the donee's position should be protected in the case of registered land by the registration of a restriction (see for example Precedent 28).

6. STEPS TO BE TAKEN

(a) Stamp Duty Land Tax

4–010 The declarations of trust will not attract SDLT and will not require a self certificate as they do not effect a transfer unless the property is subject to a debt and the beneficial owner covenants to discharge it.

(b) HM Land Registry

The entry of a Form B or Form N restriction on the register will cost £40, as will an application for registration of a caution. Entry of a Form A restriction is free as before.

(c) Copies

All interested parties in the declaration of trust should have a copy.

Precedent 21—Property purchased by nominee for person providing the purchase money.

4–011

THIS DECLARATION OF TRUST is made the   day of
          200

BETWEEN (1) [X] of   [address] ("the Trustee") and
(2) [Y] of   [address] ("the Owner")

WHEREAS:

(A) By a Conveyance/Transfer dated   made between (1) [Vendor] and (2) the Trustee the property ("the Property") details of which are contained in the Schedule was conveyed/transferred to the Trustee

(B) The entirety of the purchase monies mentioned in the Conveyance/Transfer and the costs relating to the Conveyance/Transfer were provided by the Owner

(C) Since the date of the Conveyance/Transfer the Property has been held by the Trustee as trustee for the Owner

NOW THIS DEED WITNESSES as follows:

1 The Trustee hereby DECLARES that he holds the Property UPON TRUST for the Owner absolutely and that he will convey the Property to the Owner or to such other person or persons as the Owner shall direct and otherwise deal with the Property as the Owner shall direct.

2 The Owner hereby COVENANTS with the Trustee to indemnify him against any costs properly incurred by the Trustee in relation to the Property

   IN WITNESS etc

SCHEDULE

[description of Property]
Attestation—*[as Precedent 1]*

Precedent 22—Council house: monies provided by third party to enable purchase by existing tenant. Split of "profit" in agreed shares after repayment of discount. No mortgage.

THIS DECLARATION OF TRUST is made the   day of **4–012**
                200

BETWEEN:

(1)   of   [address] ("the Owner") and
(2)   of   [address] ("the Contributor")

1 Interpretation
In this Deed the following expressions shall have the following meanings:

1.1 "the Act"	means the Housing Act 1985 and any statutory modification or re-enactment thereof
1.2 "the Council"	means Borough Council
1.3 "the Property"	means ALL THAT freehold property situate at and known as [*insert address*]
1.4 "the Value"	means the sum of £ being the market value of the Property assessed in accordance with s.127 of the Act
1.5 "the Discount"	means the sum of £ being the Discount to which the Owner is entitled under s.129 of the Act
1.6 "the Discounted Purchase Price"	means the sum of £ paid by the Owner for the Property being the Value less the Discount
1.7 "the Contribution"	means the sum of £ paid by the Contributor as a contribution to the Discounted Purchase Price
1.8 "Relevant Disposal"	means a disposal of the Property falling within s.159(1) of the Act and giving rise to a repayment of the whole or part of the Discount

1.9 "the Relevant Discount"   shall mean

a) in the first year from the date of the Conveyance/Transfer a sum equal to the Discount

b) in the second year from the date of the Conveyance/Transfer a sum equal to two thirds of the Discount

c) in the third year from the date of the Conveyance/Transfer a sum equal to one third of the Discount

d) in the fourth and subsequent years from the date of the Conveyance/Transfer a sum equal to nil

1.10 "the Conveyance/Transfer   means a Conveyance/Transfer of even date but executed before these presents made between (1) the Council and (2) the Owner

1.11 "the Net Proceeds of Sale"   means the proceeds of sale of the Property together with the net rents and profits thereof until sale after deducting therefrom the costs of such sale.

2 Recitals

2.1 By the Conveyance/Transfer the Property was conveyed to the Owner for an estate in fee simple in consideration of payment of the Discounted Purchase Price

2.2 The Conveyance/Transfer contained a covenant on the part of the Owner to pay to the Council on demand an amount equal to the Relevant Discount if within a period of three years from the date of the Conveyance/Transfer there is a Relevant Disposal but if there is more than one such disposal then only on the first of them

2.3 In view of the Contribution the parties have agreed that the Property and the Net Proceeds of Sale shall be held by the Owner upon trust for the Owner and the Contributor in manner mentioned below

3 IT IS HEREBY DECLARED that with effect from this date the Owner holds the Property and the Net Proceeds of sale upon

trust for the Owner and the Contributor as tenants in common on the basis that:

3.1 the Contributor is entitled to the share of the Net Proceeds of Sale in accordance with the formula set out in the Schedule

3.2 the Owner is entitled to the balance of the Net Proceeds of Sale after deduction of the share of the Contributor above

4 IT IS HEREBY AGREED that

4.1 The Owner shall be entitled to occupy the Property rent free for as long as she shall wish and that the power of sale shall not be exercised without her consent.

4.2 During such occupation the Owner shall keep the Property in a reasonable state of repair and condition and shall insure the same for not less than the Value against damage by fire and other risks normally insured against and under a policy of insurance in respect of a private dwelling-house.

4.3 During such occupation the Owner shall not allow any person to share occupation of the Property upon terms that would enable any tenancy or security of tenure or interest in the Property or its proceeds of sale to be obtained by such person.

IN WITNESS whereof this deed has been duly executed the day and year first before written

SCHEDULE

The share of the Net Proceeds of Sale of the Contributor shall be ascertained by

i) taking the Net Proceeds of Sale and

ii) in the first second or third year from the date of the Conveyance/Transfer deducting therefrom the Relevant Discount and

iii) then taking off an amount equivalent to the Contribution and paying that to the Contributor (or if there are not sufficient monies to equal the Contribution the balance remaining) and holding [50%] of the balance for the Contributor.

SIGNED and DELIVERED AS
A DEED by the Owner in
the presence of:

SIGNED and DELIVERED AS
A DEED by the Contributor
in the presence of:

Precedent 23—Council house: monies provided by Contributor to enable purchase by existing tenant. Split of "profit" in agreed shares after repayment of discount. Mortgage granted to existing tenant who remains responsible for same.

THIS DECLARATION OF TRUST is made the   day of **4–013**
          200

BETWEEN: (1)   of   [address] ("the Owner") and (2)   of   [address] ("the Contributor")

1 Interpretation
In this deed the following expressions shall have the following meanings: [*take in Precedent 22, clauses 1.1 to 1.10 inclusive*]

1.11	"the Net Proceeds of Sale"	means the proceeds of sale of the Property together with the net rents and profits thereof until sale after deducting therefrom the costs of such sale, and after repayment of the Mortgage
1.12	"the Mortgage"	means the sum secured by a Legal Charge over the Property in favour of [*Building Society*] being originally £ or such sum from time to time outstanding thereunder

2 Recitals
[*as Precedent 22, clause 2*]

3 IT IS HEREBY DECLARED that with effect from this date the Owner holds the Property and the Net Proceeds of Sale upon trust for the Owner and the Contributor as tenants in common on the basis that:
3.1 the Contributor is entitled to the share of the Net Proceeds of Sale in accordance with the formula set out in the Schedule
3.2 the Owner is entitled to the balance of the Net Proceeds of Sale after deduction of the share of the Contributor above

4 IT IS HEREBY AGREED that
4.1 The Owner shall be entitled to occupy the Property rent free for so long as she shall wish and that the power of sale shall not be exercised without her consent.

4.2 During such occupation the Owner shall not allow any person to share occupation of the Property upon terms that would enable any tenancy or security of tenure or interest in the Property or its proceeds of sale to be obtained by such person.

4.3 The Owner shall be liable to make all payments due under the Mortgage and shall observe the terms and conditions thereof and indemnifies the Contributor accordingly.

IN WITNESS whereof this deed has been duly executed the day and year first before written

SCHEDULE

The share of the Net Proceeds of Sale of the Contributor shall be ascertained by

   i) taking the Net Proceeds of Sale and

   ii) in the first second or third year from the date of the Conveyance/Transfer deducting therefrom the Relevant Discount and

   iii) then taking off an amount equivalent to the Contribution and paying that to the Contributor (or if there are not sufficient monies to equal the Contribution the balance remaining) and holding [50%] of the balance for the Contributor

SIGNED and DELIVERED
AS A DEED by the Owner in the
presence of:

SIGNED and DELIVERED AS
A DEED by the Contributor
in the presence of:

Precedent 24—Council house: monies provided by third party. Benefit of occupier's share held for grandchildren.

THIS DECLARATION OF TRUST is made the   day of **4–014**
          2000

BETWEEN: (1)   of   [address] ("the Owner") and (2)   of   [address] ("the Contributor")

1 Interpretation
In this deed the following expressions shall have the following meanings:
[*take in Precedent 22 clauses 1.1 to 1.11 inclusive*]

2 Recitals
2.1 [Precedent 22 clause 2.1]
2.2 [Precedent 22 clause 2.2]
2.3 The parties have agreed that the Property shall be held by the Owner upon the trusts set out hereafter.

3 IT IS HEREBY DECLARED that with effect from this date the Owner holds the Property and the Net Proceeds of Sale upon trust for the Owner and the Contributor as tenants in common on the basis that
3.1 the Contributor is entitled to the share of the Net Proceeds of Sale in accordance with the formula set out in the Schedule
3.2 the balance thereof shall be held for X and Y (being the grandchildren of the Owner) in equal shares

4 [Precedent 22 clause 4]

5 IT IS HEREBY AGREED AND DECLARED by the parties hereto that the power of appointing new Trustees of this Deed shall be vested in [the Contributor]

6 THE statutory powers of maintenance accumulation and advancement shall apply to the trusts declared herein but so that the power of maintenance shall be exercisable as the Trustees shall think fit and free from any obligation to apply a proportionate part only of income where other income is applicable for maintenance purposes and the power of advancement shall authorise the application of the whole or any part (instead of being limited to one half) of the share or interest of a beneficiary hereunder

7 IN the event that any of the persons named in clause 3.2 hereof shall be a minor the Trustees shall have power to pay any monies to which such minor is entitled to the parent or guardian of such minor whose receipt shall be a good discharge to the Trustees

IN WITNESS etc

SCHEDULE

[*as Precedent 22*]

SIGNED and DELIVERED
as a DEED by the Owner
in the presence of:

SIGNED and DELIVERED
as a DEED by the
Contributor in the
presence of:

Precedent 25—Retirement of council occupier as trustee of the Declaration.

THIS DEED OF RETIREMENT AND APPOINTMENT OF **4–015**
NEW TRUSTEES is made this   day of   200
BETWEEN: (1) [*The Owner*] of   [address] ("the
Retiring Trustee") (2) [*The Contributor and parent of grandchild*]
of   [address] ("the New Trustees")

WHEREAS:

(A) By a Declaration of Trust ("the Declaration") dated
           and made by the Retiring Trustee and the [*Contributor*] trusts were declared concerning the Property described in the
Schedule and the net proceeds of sale thereof

(B) The power of appointing new trustees of the Declaration was
vested in the Contributor under clause (   ) thereof

(C) The Retiring Trustee wishes to be discharged from the trusts
of the Declaration

(D) The Contributor wishes to appoint the New Trustees to be
trustees of the trusts of the Declaration in place of the Retiring
Trustee

NOW THIS DEED WITNESSES that in exercise of the power in
that behalf vested in him by the Declaration and of every other
power him enabling the Contributor APPOINTS the New
Trustees to be trustees of the Declaration in the place of the
Retiring Trustee who hereby retires.

   IN WITNESS etc

SCHEDULE

[*description of Property*]

Attestation—[*as Precedent 1*]

Precedent 26—Property in sole name of one party subject to mortgage. Declaration of trust that property held for self and another in specified shares.

4–016 THIS DECLARATION OF TRUST is made this   day of
            200
BETWEEN (1) [X] of   [address] ("the Legal Owner")
and (2) [Y] of   [address] ("the Contributor")
WHEREAS:

(A) By a Transfer dated   the property ("the Property") details of which are contained in the Schedule was transferred to the Legal Owner

(B) By a Mortgage ("the Mortgage") dated the same date as the transfer the Legal Owner charged the Property to the [*Building Society*] to secure the sum of £

(C) The purchase money for the Property was provided by the Legal Owner and the Contributor in the shares and proportions hereinafter mentioned and the Property was transferred to the Legal Owner who confirms that he holds the same as trustee for himself and the Contributor

NOW THIS DEED WITNESSES as follows:

1 The Legal Owner declares that he holds the Property and the net proceeds of sale (after deducting therefrom the costs of sale but not the balance of any money due under the Mortgage) and the net rents and profits until sale UPON TRUST for the Legal Owner and the Contributor as tenants in common

   (a) as to 41/56ths for the Legal Owner absolutely

   (b) as to 15/56ths for the Contributor absolutely

2 The Legal Owner charges his said share in the Property with the payment of all monies secured by the Mortgage in exoneration of the Contributor's share in the Property

3 The Legal Owner hereby covenants with the Contributor that he will pay all monies secured by and payable under the Mortgage and will at all times hereafter indemnify and keep indemnified the Contributor and his estate and effects from all actions proceedings costs claims and demands in respect thereof

4 The Legal Owner hereby covenants with the Contributor that he will not create any further mortgages or otherwise deal with or dispose of all or any part of the Property without the consent in writing of the Contributor

IN WITNESS etc

SCHEDULE

[*description of Property*]

Attestation—[*as Precedent 1*]

Precedent 27—Property in sole name of wife subject to mortgage. Declaration of trust recognises the contribution of husband by way of improvements to the property. Power of sale limited during lifetime of survivor.

4–017 THIS DECLARATION OF TRUST is made this   day of   200

BY   of   [*address*] ("the Owner") and to which [*the Contributor*] ("(the Contributor") of [*address*]

is a party to show his acceptance of the terms hereof

WHEREAS:

(A) The Owner is the registered proprietor of the property ("the Property") details of which are contained in the Schedule

(B) Since the acquisition of the Property in her then name of [   ] the Owner has married the Contributor

(C) The Contributor has expended substantial monies on the Property and it is agreed between the Owner and the Contributor that the Property (subject to the existing Mortgage in favour of [*Building Society*]) should be held as to three-fifths for the Owner and two-fifths for the Contributor or their respective Estates

NOW IT IS HEREBY DECLARED as follows:

1 The Owner declares that she holds the Property and the net proceeds of sale thereof (after deduction of the costs of sale) and the net rents and profits until sale upon trust for the Owner and the Contributor as tenants in common as to three-fifths for the Owner and two-fifths for the Contributor

2 It is agreed between the Owner and the Contributor that any Mortgage on the Property should be deducted from the net proceeds of sale before any division thereof

3 It is agreed between the Owner and the Contributor that neither of them nor their respective personal representatives can force a sale of the Property during the lifetime of either of them

4 It is agreed that a restriction will be registered at HM Land Registry to the effect that the Owner cannot sell the Property without the consent of the Contributor during his lifetime or the consent of his personal representatives following his death

5 It is agreed between the Owner and the Contributor that this Declaration shall be binding upon their respective Personal Representatives

IN WITNESS whereof the Owner and the Contributor have duly executed this Declaration the day and year first before written

SCHEDULE

[description of Property]

Attestation—[as Precedent 1]

Precedent 28—Application by beneficiary to register a form A restriction under LRA 2002 s.43(1)(c) and LRR 2003 Rule 93(a).

| Application to enter a restriction | Land Registry | **RX1** |

4–018 *If you need more room than is provided for in a panel, use continuation sheet CS and attach to this form.*

---

1. Administrative area and postcode if known   [AREA]

2. Title number(s) [TITLE NUMBER]

3. If you have already made this application by **outline application,** insert reference number:

4. Property *Insert address or other description.*
[ADDRESS]
The restriction applied for is to affect *Place "X" in the appropriate box and complete as necessary.*

☒ the whole of each registered estate

☐ the part(s) of the registered estate(s) shown on the attached plan by *State reference e.g. "edged red".*

☐ the registered charge(s) dated   in favour of
            referred to in the Charges Register

5. Application and fee *A fee calculator for all types of applications can be found on Land Registry's website at www.landregistry.gov.uk/fees*

Restriction   Fee paid £

Fee payment method: *Place "X" in the appropriate box.*

I wish to pay the appropriate fee payable under the current Land Registration Fee Order:

☐ by cheque or postal order, amount £_____ made payable to "Land Registry".

☐ by Direct Debit under an authorised agreement with Land Registry.

| FOR OFFICIAL USE ONLY |
| Record of fee paid |
| Particulars of under/over payment |
| Fees debited £ |
| Reference number |

6. Documents lodged with this application *If this application is accompanied by either Form AP1 or FR1 please only complete the corresponding panel on Form AP1 or DL. Number the documents in sequence; copies should also be numbered and listed as separate documents, alternatively you may prefer to use Form DL. If you supply the original document and a certified copy, we shall assume that you request the return of the original; if a certified copy is not supplied, we may retain the original document and it may be destroyed.*

Declaration of trust dated [   ] made by [X] and certified copy of the same

7. The applicant is: *Please provide the full name of the person applying for the restriction.*
[Y] (BENEFICIAL OWNER)

The application has been lodged by:
Land Registry Key No. (if appropriate)
Name (if different from the applicant)
Address/DX No.   [ADDRESS]

Reference
E-mail

Telephone No. | Fax No.

| FOR OFFICIAL USE ONLY |
| Codes |
| Dealing |
| Status |

8. Where you would like us to deal with someone else *We shall deal only with the applicant, or the person lodging the application if different, unless you place "X" against one or more of the statements below and give the necessary details.*

☐ Send title information document to the person shown below

☐ Raise any requisitions or queries with the person shown below

☐ Return original documents lodged with this form (see note in panel 6) to the person shown below
  If this applies only to certain documents, please specify.

Name
Address/DX No.

Reference
E-mail

Telephone No.	Fax No.

9. Entitlement to apply for a restriction *Place "X" in the appropriate box.*

☒ The applicant is the registered proprietor of the registered estate/charge referred to in panel 4.

☐ The applicant is the person **entitled** to be registered as proprietor of the registered estate/charge referred to in panel 4. **Complete panel 12.**

☐ The consent of the registered proprietor of the registered estate/charge referred to in panel 4 accompanies this application or the applicant's conveyancer certifies that he holds this consent. **Complete panel 11.**

☐ The consent of the person **entitled** to be registered as proprietor of the registered estate/charge referred to in panel 4 accompanies this application or the applicant's conveyancer certifies that he holds this consent. **Complete panels 11 and 12.**

☒ Evidence that the applicant has sufficient interest in the making of the entry of the restriction applied for in panel 10 accompanies this application. **Complete panel 13.**

10. The applicant applies to enter the following restriction against the registered estate/charge referred to in panel 4: *Please set out the form of restriction required. Schedule 4 to the Land Registration Rules 2003 contains standard forms of restrictions. Use this form to apply for a standard form of restriction (as set out in Schedule 4 to the Land Registration Rules 2003) or, where appropriate, a restriction in another form. If the restriction is not a standard form of restriction, the registrar must be satisfied that the terms of the proposed restriction are reasonable and that applying the proposed restriction would be straightforward and not place an unreasonable burden on him. If the restriction requires notice to be given to a person, requires a person's consent or certificate or is a standard form restriction that refers to a named person, include that person's address for service.*

No disposition by a sole proprieter of the registered estate (except a trust corporation) under which capital money arises is to be registered unless authorised by an order of the court.

11. Evidence of consent *Please complete this panel if instructed to do so in panel 9. Place "X" in the appropriate box.*

☐ The [registered proprietor of][person entitled to be registered as the proprietor of] the registered estate/charge referred to in panel 4 consents to the entry of the restriction and that person or their conveyancer has completed panel 15.

☐ I am the applicant's conveyancer and certify that I hold the consent referred to in panel 9.

☐ The consent referred to in panel 9 is contained on page ____ of the document numbered ____ referred to in [panel 6][Form AP1][Form DL].

12. Evidence of entitlement to be registered as proprietor *Please complete this panel if instructed to do so in panel 9. Place "X" in the appropriate box.*

☐ I am the applicant's conveyancer and certify that I am satisfied that the applicant/person consenting to this application is entitled to be registered as proprietor and that I hold the originals of the documents that contain evidence of that person's entitlement, or an application for registration of that person as proprietor is pending at Land Registry.

☐ Evidence that the applicant/person consenting to this application is entitled to be registered as proprietor is contained in the document(s) numbered ____ referred to in [panel 6][Form AP1][Form DL].

13. Evidence that the applicant has sufficient interest *Please complete this panel if instructed to do so in panel 9.*

State brief details of the applicant's interest in the making of the entry of the restriction applied for in panel 10.

The applicant has interest in the property as set out in LRR 2003 Rule 93(a) under a declaration of trust dated [   ] and made by [X] of [address] (the legal owner).

Evidence of this interest is contained in the document(s) numbered referred to in [panel 6][Form AP1][Form DL].

14. Signature of applicant

or their conveyancer _____ **Date** _____

15. Consent
Consent to the entry of the restriction specified in panel 10 is given by:

Names *BLOCK LETTERS*	**Signatures**
1.	1.
2.	2.
3.	3.

© Crown copyright (ref: LR/HQ) 6/03

Precedent 29—Application by beneficiary to register a form N restriction

**Application to enter
a restriction**

Land Registry

RX1

If you need more room than is provided for in a panel, use continuation sheet CS and attach to this form. **4–019**

1. Administrative area and postcode if known [AREA]
2. Title number(s) [TITLE NUMBER]

3. If you have already made this application by **outline application,**
insert reference number:

4. Property *Insert address or other description.*
[ADDRESS]
The restriction applied for is to affect *Place "X" in the appropriate box and complete as necessary.*

☒ the whole of each registered estate

☐ the part(s) of the registered estate(s) shown on the attached plan by *State reference e.g. "edged red".*

☐ the registered charge(s) dated   in favour of
                                    referred to in the Charges Register

5. Application and fee *A fee calculator for all types of applications can be found on Land Registry's website at www.landregistry.gov.uk/fees*

Restriction   Fee paid £   40

Fee payment method: *Place "X" in the appropriate box.*

I wish to pay the appropriate fee payable under the current Land Registration Fee Order:

☐ by cheque or postal order, amount £_____ made payable to "Land Registry".

☐ by Direct Debit under an authorised agreement with Land Registry.

FOR OFFICIAL USE ONLY
Record of fee paid

Particulars of under/over payment

Fees debited £

Reference number

6. Documents lodged with this application *If this application is accompanied by either Form AP1 or FR1 please only complete the corresponding panel on Form AP1 or DL. Number the documents in sequence; copies should also be numbered and listed as separate documents, alternatively you may prefer to use Form DL. If you supply the original document and a certified copy, we shall assume that you request the return of the original; if a certified copy is not supplied, we may retain the original document and it may be destroyed.*

Declaration of trust dated [   ] made by [X] and certified copy of the same

7. The applicant is: *Please provide the full name of the person applying for the restriction.*
[Y] [BENEFICIAL OWNER]

The application has been lodged by:
Land Registry Key No. (if appropriate)
Name (if different from the applicant)
Address/DX No.   [ADDRESS]

Reference
E-mail

Telephone No.   Fax No.

FOR
OFFICIAL
USE ONLY
Codes
Dealing

Status

---

8. **Where you would like us to deal with someone else** *We shall deal only with the applicant, or the person lodging the application if different, unless you place "X" against one or more of the statements below and give the necessary details.*

☐ Send title information document to the person shown below

☐ Raise any requisitions or queries with the person shown below

☐ Return original documents lodged with this form (see note in panel 6) to the person shown below
If this applies only to certain documents, please specify.

Name
Address/DX No.

Reference
E-mail

Telephone No.	Fax No.

9. **Entitlement to apply for a restriction** *Place "X" in the appropriate box.*

☐ The applicant is the registered proprietor of the registered estate/charge referred to in panel 4.

☐ The applicant is the person **entitled** to be registered as proprietor of the registered estate/charge referred to in panel 4. **Complete panel 12.**

☐ The consent of the registered proprietor of the registered estate/charge referred to in panel 4 accompanies this application or the applicant's conveyancer certifies that he holds this consent. **Complete panel 11.**

☐ The consent of the person **entitled** to be registered as proprietor of the registered estate/charge referred to in panel 4 accompanies this application or the applicant's conveyancer certifies that he holds this consent. **Complete panels 11 and 12.**

☒ Evidence that the applicant has sufficient interest in the making of the entry of the restriction applied for in panel 10 accompanies this application. **Complete panel 13.**

10. **The applicant applies to enter the following restriction against the registered estate/charge referred to in panel 4:** *Please set out the form of restriction required. Schedule 4 to the Land Registration Rules 2003 contains standard forms of restrictions. Use this form to apply for a standard form of restriction (as set out in Schedule 4 to the Land Registration Rules 2003) or, where appropriate, a restriction in another form. If the restriction is not a standard form of restriction, the registrar must be satisfied that the terms of the proposed restriction are reasonable and that applying the proposed restriction would be straightforward and not place an unreasonable burden on him. If the restriction requires notice to be given to a person, requires a person's consent or certificate or is a standard form restriction that refers to a named person, include that person's address for service.*

No disposition of the registered estate by the proprietor of the registered estate is to be registered without a written consent signed by [Y] of [address].

11. Evidence of consent *Please complete this panel if instructed to do so in panel 9. Place "X" in the appropriate box.*

☐ The [registered proprietor of][person entitled to be registered as the proprietor of] the registered estate/charge referred to in panel 4 consents to the entry of the restriction and that person or their conveyancer has completed panel 15.

☐ I am the applicant's conveyancer and certify that I hold the consent referred to in panel 9.

☐ The consent referred to in panel 9 is contained on page ____ of the document numbered _____ referred to in [panel 6][Form AP1][Form DL].

12. Evidence of entitlement to be registered as proprietor *Please complete this panel if instructed to do so in panel 9. Place "X" in the appropriate box.*

☐ I am the applicant's conveyancer and certify that I am satisfied that the applicant/person consenting to this application is entitled to be registered as proprietor and that I hold the originals of the documents that contain evidence of that person's entitlement, or an application for registration of that person as proprietor is pending at Land Registry.

☐ Evidence that the applicant/person consenting to this application is entitled to be registered as proprietor is contained in the document(s) numbered ____ referred to in [panel 6][Form AP1][Form DL].

13. Evidence that the applicant has sufficient interest *Please complete this panel if instructed to do so in panel 9.*

State brief details of the applicant's interest in the making of the entry of the restriction applied for in panel 10.

The applicant has an interest in the property as set out in LRR 2003 Rule 93(a) under a declaration of trust dated [   ] and made by [X] of [address] (the legal owner).

Evidence of this interest is contained in the document(s) numbered referred to in [panel 6] [Form AP1][Form DL].

14. Signature of applicant

or their conveyancer _____ **Date** _____

15. Consent
Consent to the entry of the restriction specified in panel 10 is given by:

Names BLOCK LETTERS	Signatures
1.	1.
2.	2.
3.	3.

Precedent 30—House in sole name, subject to mortgage. Equity henceforward held for another. Transferor remaining liable on mortgage.

4–020 THIS DECLARATION OF TRUST is made the day of 200
BETWEEN (1) [*X*] of [*address*] ("the Trustee") and (2) [*Y*] of [*address*] ("the Beneficiary")

WHEREAS:

(A) The Trustee is the registered proprietor of the property ("the Property") details of which are given in the schedule hereto subject to a charge ("the Registered Charge") in favour of [*National Westminster Home Loans Limited*]

(B) The Trustee is desirous of holding the Property subject to the Registered Charge UPON TRUST for the Beneficiary absolutely

NOW THIS DEED WITNESSES as follows:

1 The Trustee hereby DECLARES that henceforward he holds the Property subject to the Registered Charge UPON TRUST for the Beneficiary absolutely and that he will sell transfer assign or otherwise deal with the Property as the Beneficiary shall direct Subject always to the provisions of the Registered Charge

2 The Trustee hereby covenants with the Beneficiary that he will continue to pay all monthly and other payments for which he is liable under the Registered Charge

IN WITNESS etc

SCHEDULE

[*description of Property*]

Attestation—[*as Precedent 1*]

5

Insurance policies

1. INTRODUCTION

It is quite common for an insurance policy to be taken out under **5–001** trusts ab initio, for instance written under the Married Women's Property Act 1882 for the benefit of a spouse (to include from December 5, 2005 a civil partner under the Civil Partnerships Act 2004), or more usually for the benefit of children to provide monies for inheritance tax purposes. Most insurance companies now provide standard forms for this purpose on request and the trusts are incorporated into the policy document.

However, it is also not unusual for a policy holder to have effected a policy on his own life for his own benefit (for instance an endowment policy which might have been taken out with a maturity date to coincide with expected payment of school fees or merely as a savings vehicle) and for that policy then to become surplus to requirements. Certainly there seems little point these days in an elderly client retaining a Whole Life with Profits policy in his own estate, as it will be subject to Inheritance Tax on his death if the estate exceeds the nil rate band (£275,000 for 2005/6). Such policies can be assigned by the policyholder by way of gift **5–002** (or even by way of sale if money needs to be raised) to a named beneficiary or to trustees; Law of Property Act 1925, s.136 (see Practical Trust Precedents (Sweet and Maxwell) Precedent (E5c1).

Alternatively the policyholder can declare that he holds the policy upon trusts as set out in a declaration of trust. Obviously in this latter case the policyholder becomes the sole trustee and it would be sensible to have a deed of appointment of trustees as soon as possible following the declaration of trust so that there are outside trustees available to claim the policy proceeds at the appropriate time (see Precedents 32 and 36). Precedent 31 is an example of a simple trust in favour of the policyholder's children although it is common to declare more complex trusts (see Practical Trust Precedents section D).

2. THE CONTENTS OF THE DECLARATION OF TRUST/ASSIGNMENT

(a) Bonuses/profits

5–003   It is presumed in all cases that the settlor would wish to settle not only the sum assured but all bonuses and profits accruing thereto. Often the most valuable portion of policy proceeds is the terminal bonus where a policy is one of long standing.

(b) Debts

The policy may already be charged (sometimes in favour of the insurance company itself to secure a loan) and it is important to be clear who is to have the responsibility for discharging such indebtedness.

(c) Payment of premiums

5–004   In a voluntary settlement it would not be usual for the settlor donor to covenant to continue to pay any premiums. After all, the beauty of policies taken out for IHT purposes is that the settlor has the flexibility of discontinuing payment of the premiums if circumstances change (the policy becoming either paid up or the donees themselves paying the premiums). However, it is useful to have an acknowledgement that any premiums paid by the settlor do not create a lien in his favour for the same.

(d) Covenant for title

The covenants for title that we associate with real property conveyances and transfers are not limited to land alone. From July 1, 1995 the Law of Property (Miscellaneous Provisions) Act 1994 introduced covenants "with full title guarantee" or "with limited title guarantee". Covenants are only implied if the key words are used. As the circumstances envisaged here are those of gift, it is inappropriate for any covenants to be implied.

(e) Covenant not to render the policy void

5–005   Such a covenant would be normal in a commercial assignment (e.g. on a matrimonial division of assets), but would not usually be included in a voluntary situation. However, if included, and the settlor for instance takes up motor racing in breach of the terms of the policy, then there would be a right of action by the trustees against him or his estate (Re Jewell's Settlement, *Watts v Public Trustee* [1919] 2 Ch. 161).

(f) Powers

It is always prudent for trustees to have power to surrender the **5–006** policy and deal generally with it so that they have maximum flexibility of action to cope with unanticipated events (for instance power to convert the policy to be paid up should the settlor cease to pay premiums, or power to lodge the policy by way of security for a loan to a beneficiary).

3. PENSION DEATH BENEFITS

Retirement annuity policies taken out by the self-employed under **5–007** s.226 Income and Corporation Taxes Act 1970 (now ICTA 1988 section 620) and personal pension policies taken out under ICTA 1988 Chapter IV provide the policy holder with two distinct benefits, an annuity at retirement and a lump sum death benefit if death occurs before retirement. In some post Finance Act 1995 policies the purchase of the annuity and payment of the death benefit may be deferred past retirement age and income withdrawn in the meantime.

It will be appreciated that the death benefits under these policies may be very valuable and in many cases, if no action is taken, will become payable to the policyholder's estate with the result that (subject to the estate exceeding the nil rate band, £275,000 for 2005/6) they will be subject to Inheritance Tax. It is prudent to arrange for these death benefits to fall outside the policy holders estate. However because the right to the annuity and the death benefit comprise a single chose in action, it is not possible to transfer the death benefit alone. Nor is any assignment of the annuities permitted. The policyholder should therefore declare himself a trustee of both elements but provide that the annuities will be paid to him or whoever is entitled under the terms of the policy. This is thought to be effective to avoid both a reservation of benefit for Inheritance tax and a charge to income tax under the pre owned assets regime. A further trustee should be appointed in the declaration itself or in a separate deed of appointment. Declaring such a trust has the advantage that

5–008

1 the death benefit payment can be made to trustees of the policy without the necessity of having to wait for a grant of probate to the policyholder's estate; and

2 if at the time of declaring the trust the policyholder is in normal health for his age, it is understood that the Revenue will treat the gift as a nominal transfer of value for IHT purposes. This treatment rests upon correspondence between the Revenue and the Association of British Insurers and indications from IR Capital Taxes (formerly the Capital Taxes Office), see Tolley's Inheritance Tax 2004/5, p.352 and Capital Taxes Guidance Note published in Trusts and Estates Tax Journal,September 2001, p.16 .

If a policyholder in a state of serious ill-health settles an existing policy, the Revenue may wish to raise a claim for IHT (see IHTA s.3(3)), particularly if larger than usual premiums were subsequently paid into the policy. However enquiries are not generally made as to the policy holder's state of health provided that he survives two years and IR Capital Taxes have indicated that they will not pursue a claim even in these circumstances where the benefit is paid to the policyholder's spouse or dependants.

5–009 The disadvantages to declaring a trust of the death benefits are that

1 once the beneficiaries are named, it is not possible to change them (although a discretionary trust does offer some flexibility)

2 once an additional trustee is appointed it is not possible for the policy to remove him (other than in the circumstances set out in Trustee Act 1925, s.36) unless specific provisions as to removal are included in the declaration.

Before entering into a declaration of trust it is essential to check the policy to see that it permits assignment of the death benefit. In the case of retirement annuities, some policies predating Finance Act 1980 may need to be endorsed by the company to allow assignment. Other policies already allow assignment to any trust whilst yet others will prohibit assignments to trusts where the policyholder or his estate could benefit.

In the case of personal pensions there are many variations in the way in which death benefits are treated and some policies already provide for the death benefits to be held automatically on discretionary trusts so that they are not capable of assignment. In such cases the insurance company will usually ask the policyholder to complete a letter of wishes indicating how the death benefit should be dealt with. To ensure that any declaration made is fully effective there is no alternative but to examine each individual policy carefully, which, if the policyholder has a portfolio of policies, could be a laborious task.

The precedents that follow either:

1 settle the death benefit of the policy for named beneficiaries (Precedent 34); or

2 settle the death benefit of the policy upon discretionary trusts on the basis that an appointment of the trust fund is made within two years of the policyholder's death (Precedent 35). If the death benefit is settled on discretionary trusts and is appointed out absolutely or on life interest or accumulation and maintenance trusts or on maintenance trusts within the two years period the Revenue regard Inheritance Tax Act 1984, ss.58(1)(d) and s.151 as applying so that no charge to Inheritance Tax arises.

4. STEPS TO BE TAKEN FOLLOWING THE DECLARATION

(a) Stamp Duty

From December 1, 2003, Stamp Duty only applies to instruments **5–010** relating to stock or marketable securities (Finance Act 2003, s.125). Therefore there is no Stamp Duty payable in respect of a declaration of trust of a life policy or pension death benefit and no Stamp Duty certificate is needed. Similarly a deed of appointment of new trustees of such is not subject to Stamp Duty and requires no certificate.

(b) Notice of assignment (Precedent 33)

No assignee of a life policy can sue an insurance company for **5–011** policy monies until notice of assignment has been given and such notice should specify the date and purpose of the assignment

(Policies of Assurance Act 1867, s.3). Notice of the declaration and appointment of trustees or of any assignment should therefore be given to the insurance company—in practice it is found that they do now require to see (and sometimes retain) the original documents.

PRECEDENTS

Precedent 31—Declaration of trust of life policy by way of gift for benefit of children.

THIS DECLARATION OF TRUST is made this   day of **5–012**
            200
by [*name*] of   [*address*] ("the Settlor")

WHEREAS:

(A) The Settlor is the beneficial owner of the Policy ("the Policy") details of which are given in the Schedule hereto

(B) The Settlor wishes to settle the Policy for the benefit of his children (all of whom are of full age) as herein appears

NOW IT IS HEREBY DECLARED as follows:

1 Henceforth the Settlor HOLDS the Policy and all monies assured by or to become payable thereunder and all benefits and advantages attaching to it (or any policy or policies substituted for the same) UPON TRUST for his children X Y and Z in equal shares absolutely.

2 The Settlor acknowledges that in so far as he pays any further premium in respect of the Policy he claims no lien on the Policy in respect of such payment.

   IN WITNESS whereof this Declaration has been duly executed the day and year before written

SCHEDULE

Life Assured   [*The Settlor*]
Policy No
Assurance Company
Sum Assured
When payable
Date of Policy
Premium   [*per month/per annum*]

SIGNED and DELIVERED
as a DEED by the Settlor
in the presence of:

Precedent 32—Deed of Appointment of Trustees of a Declaration of Trust. Settlor ceasing to be a trustee.

THIS DEED OF APPOINTMENT AND RETIREMENT is **5–013** made this day of 200
BETWEEN:
(1) [*The Settlor*] of [*address*] ("the Appointor") and
(2) X of [*address*] Y of [*address*] and Z of [*address*] ("the New Trustees")

WHEREAS:

(A) The Appointor is the sole trustee of a Declaration of Trust dated ("the Declaration") made by the Appointor in relation to a Policy details of which are given in the Schedule hereto

(B) The Appointor wishes to appoint the New Trustees to be trustees of the Declaration and himself to retire as a trustee thereof

NOW THIS DEED WITNESSES as follows:

In exercise of the power given to him by the Trustee Act 1925 and of every other power him enabling the Appointor hereby APPOINTS the New Trustees to be trustees of the Declaration in place of the Appointor who hereby retires as a trustee thereof

   IN WITNESS etc

SCHEDULE

[*take in details of the Policy from Declaration*]

Attestation by all parties

Precedent 33—Notice of Declaration of Trust and Appointment of Trustees to Assurance Company.

5–014 To [*Assurance Company—name and address*]
Policy No [   ]
Life Assured[   ]

As Solicitors for and on behalf of X Y and Z we hereby give you notice that:

(a) by a Declaration of Trust dated   made by [*Settlor*] the above policy was declared to be subject to the trusts thereof

(b) by a Deed of Appointment and Retirement dated [   ] X Y and Z were appointed trustees of the Declaration and [*Settlor*] retired as a trustee thereof

A copy certified by us to be a true copy of each document referred to above is enclosed.

Please acknowledge receipt by signing and returning the duplicate of this notice enclosed.

Dated [*insert date*]

Signed [*insert name and address of Solicitors*]

Precedent 34—Declaration of trust (coupled with an appointment of trustees) of retirement annuity policy or personal pension policy

THIS DECLARATION OF TRUST is made the   day of **5–015**
    200

BETWEEN:

(1) of   [address] ("the Settlor") and (2) the Settlor and
X of   [address]
and Y of   [address] ("the Trustees" which expression shall include the trustee or trustees for the time being hereof)

WHEREAS:

(A) The Settlor is the beneficial owner of the policy ("the Policy") details of which are set out in the Schedule

(B) The Settlor wishes to declare trusts in respect of the Policy and appoint X and Y as additional trustees of the Policy which office they have agreed to accept

NOW THIS DEED WITNESSES as follows:

1 In this Declaration the following expressions shall have the following meanings:

    (a) "the Annuity" shall mean any annuity payable to the Settlor under the Policy including any income withdrawals which the Settlor may elect to receive in place of such annuity and any sums arising from the commutation of the annuity

    (b) "the Spouses or Dependant's Annuity" shall mean any annuity or annuities payable under the Policy and stated to be payable to the Settlor's spouse child or dependant and shall include any income withdrawals made to such a person if an election is made to receive such withdrawals in place of such annuity

    (c) "the Death Benefit" shall mean any monies payable under the Policy in the event of the death of the Settlor otherwise than in the form of an annuity or lump sum arising from the commutation of the annuity and all capital sums or investments held by the Trustees representing such benefits for the time being

2 The Settlor hereby DECLARES that he will henceforth hold the Policy and the benefits payable under it on the following trusts

3 The Settlor ACKNOWLEDGES that he alone is entitled to make payment of any future premiums under the Policy (but does not thereby undertake any obligation to pay the same) and claims no lien in respect of any such payments

4 The Trustees shall hold the Annuity upon trust for the Settlor absolutely

5 The Trustees shall hold the Spouse's or Dependant's Annuity upon trust absolutely for the person or persons named in the Policy and satisfying the conditions contained or referred to in the Policy

6 The Trustees shall hold the Death Benefit upon trust for the benefit of [*insert named beneficiaries*]

7 All income accruing in the hands of the Trustees whether before or after the death of the Settlor shall be paid or applied to or for the benefit of the individual(s) entitled for the time being to such income under the trusts hereof

8 In addition to the powers conferred by law the trustees shall have the following powers in the execution of these trusts:

(a) power to invest or apply any monies requiring investment as if they were absolute owners beneficially entitled including the power to lend money to the executors and trustees of the Settlor's Will with or without security upon such terms as they may think fit and so that the Trustees shall not be liable for any loss which may occur at any time in connection with or in consequence of any investments made under the powers hereby conferred upon them

(b) power during the minority of a beneficiary to pay or apply the income or capital to which such beneficiary may be entitled for or towards the advancement maintenance education or benefit of such beneficiary (without regard to limits otherwise imposed by statute) and to make such payments to the parents or guardians of such beneficiary for the purposes aforesaid without seeing to the application thereof and so that the receipt of such parents or guardians shall be a complete discharge to the Trustees;

9 All the rights and options contained in or allowed in connection with the Policy and exercisable by the Settlor, his spouse, children

or dependants shall continue to be exercisable by such person and such powers shall be exercisable by such person without reference or regard to the trusts hereby declared

10 Neither the Settlor nor any other of the Trustees shall be under any obligation whatsoever to keep up the Policy or to reinstate the same if it shall become void

11 The Trustees may appropriate any part of the Death Benefit in its actual state of investment and after making such valuations as the Trustees shall think fit in or towards the satisfaction of the interest of any person beneficially interested in the Death Benefit or the income thereof but without the necessity of obtaining the consent of that or of any other person

12 (a) Any Trustee (other than the Settlor) hereof being a solicitor or other person engaged in any profession or business shall be entitled to be paid all usual professional or other charges for business transacted time expended and acts done by him or his firm in connection with the trusts hereof including acts which a trustee not being in any profession or business could have done personally

(b) A corporate trustee may be appointed a trustee hereof on such terms and conditions as to remuneration and otherwise in all respects as shall be agreed at the time of appointment

13 (i) The power of appointing new or additional trustees hereof shall be vested in the Settlor during his lifetime

(ii) Any corporate body may be appointed trustee hereof on such terms and conditions as to remuneration and other-wise in all respects as the appointor shall prescribe or approve

(iii) The Settlor hereby appoints X and Y to be trustees to act with him in the trusts of this Declaration

14 In the performance of the trusts hereof no trustee shall be liable for any loss arising as a result of any act done or omission made in good faith or by reason of any mistake made by that trustee (other than a mistake which amounts to culpable wrong-doing on the part of that trustee)

15 The Trustees may at any time or times during the continuance of the trusts hereof by deed or deeds release or restrict the future exercise of all or any of the powers herein conferred on them either wholly and so as to bind their successors or to any lesser extent specified in any such deed or deeds

IN WITNESS etc

SCHEDULE

Policy No(s)
Assurance Company
Date of policy(ies)

SIGNED and delivered as a
Deed by the Settlor in
the presence of:

SIGNED and delivered as a
Deed by [*Trustee*] in the
presence of:

SIGNED and delivered as a
Deed by [*Trustee*] in the
presence of:

Precedent 35—Declaration of Trust of retirement annuity policy or personal pension policy. Discretionary trust to be exercised within two years of death.

THIS DECLARATION OF TRUST is made this   day of **5–016**
          200
BY   of   [*address*]

WHEREAS:

(A) See Precedent 34

(B) The Settlor wishes to declare trusts in respect of the Policy

NOW THIS DEED WITNESSES as follows:

1 (a)–(c) as Precedent 34
1 (d) "The Trustees" shall mean the trustees for the time being of this Declaration
2 The Settlor hereby DECLARES that he will henceforth hold the Policy and the benefits payable under it as trustee on the following trusts.
3 As Precedent 34 clause 3
4 As Precedent 34 clause 4
5 As Precedent 34 clause 5
6 The Trustees shall hold the Death Benefit UPON TRUST for such one or more exclusively or all of the following class namely:

  (i) any person to whom the Settlor shall be or shall have been married
  (ii) any child or children of the Settlor whenever born
  (iii) any grandchild or grandchildren of the Settlor whenever born
  (iv) the Settlors parents [*insert names*]
  (v) any other individual (excluding the Settlor) or any charity nominated by the Settlor by notice in writing addressed to and received by the Trustee not later than one month prior to the Settlor's death

in such shares and for such interests whether absolute or limited as the Trustees shall in their uncontrolled discretion appoint during the Settlor's lifetime or within the period of two years from the date of the Settlor's death **PROVIDED ALWAYS** that any part of the Death Benefit which shall remain unappointed as aforesaid at the end of the said period of two years shall be held by the Trustees for such of the Settlor's widow and children as are alive at that time and if more than one in equal shares but if the foregoing trusts shall fail then upon trust absolutely for such charity or charities as the Trustees shall in their absolute discretion select and for the general purposes of the same

7 All income accruing in the hands of the Trustees whether before or after the death of the Settlor shall be paid or applied to or for the benefit of the individual(s) entitled for the time being to such income under the trusts hereof.

8 In addition to the powers conferred by law the Trustees shall have the following powers in the execution of these trusts:

(a) power to invest or apply any monies requiring investment as if they were absolute owners beneficially entitled including the power to lend money to the executors and trustees of the Settlor's Will with or without security upon such terms as they may think fit and so that the Trustees shall not be liable for any loss which may occur at any time in connection with or in consequence of any investments made under the powers hereby conferred upon them

(b) power during the minority of a beneficiary to pay or apply the income or capital to which such beneficiary may be entitled for or towards the advancement maintenance education or benefit of such beneficiary (without regard to limits otherwise imposed by statute) and to make such payments to the parents or guardians of such beneficiary for the purposes aforesaid without seeing to the application thereof and so that the receipt of such parents or guardians shall be a complete discharge to the Trustees;

9 All the rights and options contained in or allowed in connection with the Policy and exercisable by the Settlor, his spouse, children or dependants shall continue to be exercisable by such person and such powers shall be exercisable by such person without reference or regard to the trusts hereby declared.

10 Neither the Settlor nor any other of the Trustees shall be under any obligation whatsoever to keep up the Policy or to reinstate the same if it shall become void.

11 The Trustees may appropriate any part of the Death Benefit in its actual state of investment and after making such valuations as the Trustees shall think fit in or towards the satisfaction of the interest of any person beneficially interested in the Death Benefit or the income thereof but without the necessity of obtaining the consent of that or of any other person

12(a) Any trustee (other than the Settlor) being a Solicitor or other person engaged in any profession or business shall be entitled to be paid all usual professional or other charges for business transacted time expended and acts done by him or his firm in connection with the trusts hereof including acts which a trustee not being in any profession or business could have done personally

(b) A corporate trustee may be appointed a trustee hereof on such terms and conditions as to remuneration and otherwise in all respects as shall be agreed at the time of appointment

13 The Trustees may as they in their absolute discretion think fit pay or apply all or any part or parts of the Death Benefit in or towards the discharge of any liabilities to Inheritance Tax or other fiscal imposition arising by reason of the Settlor's death and in respect of which the liability for such a payment would otherwise fall entirely either directly or indirectly on any one or more of the beneficiaries hereunder by reason of whatever interest any of them may have in any such property and which liability would otherwise diminish or otherwise affect their entitlement to such property PROVIDED that no such payment by the Trustees on behalf of any beneficiary as aforesaid shall exceed the value of the interest which such beneficiary has in the Death Benefit at the time of such payment by the Trustees whether absolute or contingent on any event or in possession or in remainder or in reversion

14 The Trustees may accept as a good and sufficient discharge a receipt of the Treasurer or other proper officer of a charity to whom payment is made as a good and sufficient discharge for such payment

15 In the performance of the trusts hereof no trustee shall be liable for any loss arising as a result of any act done or omission made in good faith or by reason of any mistake made by that trustee (other than a mistake which amounts to culpable wrong doing on the part of that trustee).

16 The power of appointing new or additional trustees hereof shall be vested in the Settlor during his lifetime

17 The Trustees may at any time or times during the continuance of the trusts hereof by deed or deeds release or restrict the future exercise of all or any of the powers herein conferred on them either wholly and so as to bind their successors or to any lesser extent specified in any such deed or deeds.

THE SCHEDULE

[insert details of policy/policies as Precedent 34]

IN WITNESS etc

SIGNED and
DELIVERED as a DEED by the said
[*X*] in the presence
of:

Precedent 36—Deed of appointment of trustees of a Declaration of Trust. Settlor remaining as a trustee.

THIS DEED OF APPOINTMENT is made this   day of **5–017**
        200
BETWEEN

(1) [The Settlor] of   [*address*] ("the Appointor") and
(2) X of   [*address*] and Y of   [*address*] ("the New Trustees")

WHEREAS:

(A) By a Declaration of Trust ("the Declaration") dated   200 the Appointor declared that he held the policy/ policies details of which are given in the Schedule hereto upon the trusts and subject to the powers and provisions as set out in the Declaration

(B) The Appointor wishes to appoint the New Trustees to be Trustees of the Declaration with himself

NOW THIS DEED WITNESSES as follows:

In exercise of the power given to him by the Trustee Act 1925 and of the power given to him in the Declaration the Appointor HEREBY APPOINTS the New Trustees to be trustees of the Declaration to act jointly with himself in the trusts of the same

   IN WITNESS etc

[*take in details of the Policy/ies from the Declaration*]

Attestation

6

Company shareholdings

1. Introduction

6–001 Company shares, just like so many other assets, can be the subject of a trust. The company itself is not concerned with any trusts to which its shares may be subject (Companies Act 1985, s.360); the members shown on the register of shareholders are its members, whether or not they are trustees or nominees for another.

In the case of joint shareholdings, unless the Articles of Association specify otherwise, it is the first-named holder who has the vote. (The Companies (Tables A to F) Regulations 1985 (S.I. No. 805), Table A, reg 55). If there is disagreement between joint shareholders as to how a vote should be exercised, that is not a matter which concerns the company.

As in all trusts there should be certainty as to the subject matter of the trust, otherwise it is void. Obviously if numbered shares are the subject of a trust, their identity is clear. However, the holding of a block of shares means that the shares are indistinguishable one from another. Provided that the proportion or number of shares is clear then a declaration of trust that a person is trustee for another of a proportion of the shares owned by the trustee is not void for lack of certainty (*Hunter v Moss* [1994] 1 W.L.R. 452).

2. Shares in the Subsidiary

6–002 Many companies have a subsidiary which has two shareholders, with one share (or the entire number of issued shares except for one) being held by the parent company and the remaining share being held either by the parent company and an individual (normally a director) or by the individual alone.

In such circumstances, to protect the parent company, it is appropriate that the individual shareholder should:

1 make a declaration of trust acknowledging that he holds the share for the parent company and will act in accordance with its instructions; and

2 sign a blank stock transfer form, so that the parent (who should also hold the share certificate) can transfer the shareholding at any appropriate time. Because this is a bare trust, there is no need for the individual trustee shareholder to have any specific powers or duties. He must act as instructed by the parent company beneficiary. If further emphasis is needed, the provisions of Precedent 38 can be incorporated into Precedent 37.

It should of course be mentioned that since the coming into force on July 15, 1992 of the Companies (Single Member Private Limited Companies) Regulations 1992 (S.I. No. 1699), only one member is required for a private limited liability company as opposed to the two members previously required under the provisions of the Companies Act 1985, s.24, which section rendered a sole shareholder (jointly and severally with the company) liable for its debts and liabilities.

3. THE NOMINEE/TRUSTEE SHAREHOLDER

There are many reasons why shares may be held by the registered **6–003** shareholder for someone else, whether in relation to all or part of the shareholding. The Companies Act 1985, Pt VI (as amended by the Companies Act 1989) and the Disclosure of Interests in Shares (Amendment) Regulations 1993 (S.I. No. 1819) require a disclosure of underlying ownership so far as public companies are concerned, and it is not proposed to deal with that aspect here. It should also be noted that some shares are now held in electronic form under the CREST system which operates in respect of certain listed companies.

A declaration of trust relating to shares in a private company may be appropriate:

1 where a person wishes to be an anonymous shareholder or has purchased shares from an existing shareholder and has difficulty (or a reluctance) in going onto the share register (see Precedent 39). A transfer is incomplete until registered

(*Powell v London* and Provincial Bank [1893] 2 Ch. 555). Pending registration the transferee only has an equitable title to the shares transferred to him. In general beneficial ownership passes when the transferor has done all in his power to effect a transfer, (see Re Rose, *Rose v IRC* [1952] Ch. 499. However, the facts must be looked at carefully; see *Pennington v Crampton* [2002] E.W.C.A. Civ 227 where it was held that the requirement to deliver a signed transfer to the donee could be dispensed with where it was clear that the donor intended to make an immediate gift, and commentary in Dymond's Capital Taxes, para.5.320–322 (Sweet and Maxwell). Where there is the likelihood of a company refusing or being reluctant to register a transfer, the execution of a declaration of trust can produce certainty of a change in beneficial ownership (see Re Macro (Ipswich) Limited [1994] 2 BCLC 354);

6–004   2 where shares in a private company are subject to a takeover bid from a public company, thus unlocking the value of the private company shares. The shareholder may wish to transfer some shares but may be reluctant to submit the transfer with his share certificate to the company registrar at a time when this might put the shares "in limbo" as far as acceptance of an offer is concerned. The declaration of trust (see Precedent 40) will serve the purpose of keeping the shares registered, whilst disposing of the benefit to the ultimate transferee; and

3 where there are restrictions on transfer or meetings of the board at which transfers are considered are infrequent and the proposed transferor wishes to effect a disposal before a given date or get a period of time running (appropriate for insolvency or inheritance tax purposes,see Chap. 1).

It is obviously sensible that a beneficiary of a declaration of trust of shares does receive a stock transfer form duly executed by the legal owner (and the share certificate if the whole of the transferor's shareholding is involved) so that it can be presented for registration should the need or opportunity arise.

A mere entry in a share register of a transfer of shares where there has been no physical transfer document is not sufficient to effect such a transfer (see International Credit and Investment Co (Overseas) v Adham [1994] 1 BCLC 66).

4. SETTLEMENT PROVISIONS

So far in this chapter we have dealt with cases where shares are **6–005** held absolutely for another. Settlements are a regular feature of tax planning, and shareholders may constitute themselves trustees of all or part of their shareholding by the making of a declaration of trust their legal standing on the share register does not alter (see above, p.124) but the beneficial interest in such shares will do so.

The declaration of trust will of course set out the beneficiaries thereof and the various trust powers and provisions. For the detailed drafting of such trusts, practitioners are referred to Practical Trust Precedents (Sweet and Maxwell) and Encyclopaedia of Forms and Precedents (Butterworths, 5th ed.) vol 40.

A declaration of trust may be particularly appropriate in a **6–006** private company with a restriction on transfers. For instance, the Articles of Association may permit transfers from a shareholder to his wife, or to himself and his spouse but otherwise require that shares to be transferred be first offered to other members. To effect a settlement, the shareholder could therefore transfer shares to himself and his wife (so that there are two trustees) and they could then make a declaration of trust in respect thereof. Precedent 37 merely illustrates what can be done by way of the recitals to a declaration of trust.

With the making of the settlement, the parties will need to consider whether hold over relief for CGT purposes is available and if so whether to make an election (see Chap. 1).

5. ADDITIONAL MATTERS

(a) Stamp Duty   6–007

A declaration of trust relating to shares continues to be stampable with fixed duty of £5 unless it constitutes a sale in which case ad valoreum duty will be payable at 1/2 per cent.

(b) Registration with Inland Revenue

The declaration of trust should be reported to the Inland Revenue on Form 41G (Trust).

(c) Income Tax

If husband and wife (or from December 5, 2005, civil partners under the Civil Partnership Act) own property jointly, income will be treated as arising to them equally unless an election is made (see Ch.1) for example to reflect unequal ownership under a declaration of trust. However under Finance Act 2004, s.91, income distributions from jointly owned shares in a close company held by a husband and wife will be automatically taxed according to actual ownership.

Precedent 37—Shareholding in subsidiary held in sole name of trustee for parent company.

THIS DECLARATION OF TRUST is made this   day of **6–008**
          200

BETWEEN:

(1) [*registered shareholder*] of   [*address*] ("the Trustee")
and

(2) [*parent company*] whose registered office is situated at   ("the Owner")

WHEREAS:

(A) The Owner is the beneficial owner of all the issued share capital of XYZ Limited ("the Company")

(B) The Trustee holds one share ("the Share") in the Company as nominee for the Owner

NOW THIS DEED WITNESSES as follows:

1 The Trustee hereby DECLARES that he holds the Share UPON TRUST for the Owner absolutely

2 The Owner hereby indemnifies the Trustee against costs claims or demands in respect of the Share

   IN WITNESS whereof this Declaration is duly executed the day and year before written

SIGNED and delivered as a
DEED by the Trustee in
the presence of:

The Common Seal of the
Owner was hereunto affixed
in the presence of:

or

SIGNED as a DEED by XYZ Limited
by [*name*] a Director and by
[*name*] the Secretary/or a
Director:

Precedent 38—Shareholding in subsidiary held in joint names of trustee and parent company.

6–009   THIS DECLARATION OF TRUST is made the   day of
                      200   by [*name and address of Trustee Shareholder*]
("the Trustee")

WHEREAS:

(A) The Trustee is the first named holder in respect of a shareholding of one £1.00 Ordinary Share in XYZ Limited ("XYZ") registered in the joint names of himself and ABC Limited ("ABC")

(B) The Trustee has at all times (as he hereby confirms) held his interest in the said Share ("the Shareholding") as a nominee of ABC

NOW IT IS HEREBY DECLARED as follows:

1 The Trustee hereby declares that he holds his interest in the Shareholding as nominee for ABC (which declaration shall extend to such further or additional Shares as the Trustee shall acquire in XYZ by reason of the Shareholding)

2 The Trustee will at the request of ABC or its successors in title attend all meetings of shareholders or otherwise of XYZ which he shall be entitled to attend by virtue of being the registered joint proprietor of the said Share or any of them and will vote at every such meeting in such manner as ABC or its successors in title shall direct and will if so required by ABC or its successors in title execute all proxies or other documents which shall be necessary or proper to enable ABC its successors in title or its nominees to vote at any such meeting in the place of the Trustee

3 The Trustee hereby authorises ABC or its successors in title to use or complete the Stock Transfer Form attached herewith (already signed by the Trustee) as ABC shall think fit and will execute such other document as may be necessary to effect the transfer of the Shareholding in such a manner as ABC or its successors in title shall direct

   IN WITNESS whereof this Declaration has been duly executed the day and year before written

SIGNED and delivered as a
DEED by the Trustee in the presence of:

Precedent 39—Part shareholding held as nominee for another, nominee to vote until instructed to the contrary, indemnity to nominee

THIS DECLARATION OF TRUST is made this   **6–010**
day of   200
BETWEEN:
(1) [*name and address of registered holder*] ("the Nominee")

and
(2) [*name and address of the underlying owner*] ("the Beneficial Owner")

NOW THIS DEED WITNESSES as follows:

1 Definitions
In this Deed the following words and expressions have the following meanings:

the "Company"	ABC Limited
the "Shares"	100 fully paid ordinary shares of 50p each in the capital of the Company being part of the total holding of shares registered in the name of the Nominee together with any further shares stock or other securities in the Company or in any other company which are derived from or issued in respect of such shares or which are distributed by the Company in respect of such shares or to which the Nominee, either alone or jointly with the Beneficial Owner, may hereafter become legally entitled by reason or as a result of the holding of such shares, including shares stock and other securities representing the same by reason of amalgamation reconstruction or re-organisation

2 Declaration of Trust
The Nominee hereby agrees and declares that he holds the Shares and all dividends interest bonuses bonus and rights issue shares and other distributions and benefits in respect thereof on trust for the Beneficial Owner

3 Dividends

The Nominee will promptly and fully account to the Beneficial Owner (or as he may direct) for all dividends distributions bonuses interest property and/or other benefits accrued or accruing upon the Shares at any time whilst they are registered in his name and the Beneficial Owner shall receive and subject thereto give a good discharge for all such dividends and other benefits

4 Voting

The Beneficial Owner agrees that until he shall give notice in writing to the Nominee to the contrary the Nominee shall be entitled to exercise all voting rights in respect of the Shares as the Nominee shall in his sole discretion decide without liability in any respect to the Beneficial Owner in consequence thereof

5 Indemnity

The Beneficial Owner will at all times indemnify and keep indemnified the Nominee and his personal representatives estate and effects against all liabilities which the Nominee may incur by reason of being the registered owner of the Shares and in particular will punctually make payment to the Nominee of any monies required in the exercise of any matters rights or benefits relating to the Shares which the Nominee or his personal representatives may be or become liable to pay together with all costs and expenses incurred by the Nominee in the execution of the trusts of this deed and any instrument of transfer in consequence thereof

6 Transfer

The Nominee will if and when requested by the Beneficial Owner certify that such instrument of transfer as is referred to above does not constitute a change in the beneficial ownership of the Shares subject to reasonable evidence being produced to him that the transfer is completed in favour of the Beneficial Owner or other nominee for the Beneficial Owner

7 Costs

The Beneficial Owner hereby agrees to pay the cost of the preparation of this Declaration and all stamp duties in relation thereto

IN WITNESS whereof the parties hereto have duly executed this Declaration the day and year before written

SIGNED and delivered as a
DEED by the Nominee in the
presence of:

SIGNED and delivered as a
DEED by the Beneficial Owner
in the presence of:

Precedent 40—Part shareholding being the subject of an immediate gift. Private company in course of takeover.

6–011 THIS DECLARATION OF TRUST is made the   day of 200

by [*name and address of registered holder*] ("Mr Smith")

WHEREAS:

[*Mr Smith*] is desirous of gifting to his daughter [*Elizabeth Smith*] ("Elizabeth") the property specified in the Schedule hereto

NOW IT IS HEREBY DECLARED as follows:

1 With immediate effect [*Mr Smith*] DECLARES that he holds the property specified in the Schedule hereto ("the Shares") for [*Elizabeth*] for her own absolute use and benefit

2 [*Mr Smith*] will at the request of [*Elizabeth*] execute any Transfer or other documents as may be necessary to place the Shares in her name or as she shall direct and whilst the Shares remain registered in his own name he will vote at any shareholders meetings (in respect of the Shares) in such manner as [*Elizabeth*] shall direct and will if so required by [*Elizabeth*] execute all proxies or other documents which may or shall be necessary or proper to enable [*Elizabeth*] or her nominee to vote at any such meeting in the place of Mr Smith

3 [*Elizabeth*] has executed this document to confirm her acceptance of the gift of the Shares

    IN WITNESS whereof [*Mr Smith*] and [*Elizabeth*] have duly executed this Declaration the day and year before written

THE SCHEDULE

1000 fully paid Ordinary Shares of £1.00 each in Smith (Holdings) Limited which shall include any Company succeeding to the same whether by amalgamation reconstruction takeover or re-arrangement and any Shares representing the same whether by a different capital holding in the said Company or in any other Company

SIGNED and delivered as a
DEED by [*Mr Smith*] in the
presence of:

SIGNED and delivered as a
DEED by [*Elizabeth*] in the
presence of:

Precedent 41—Declaration of trust of company shares already held in the names of the trustees. Commencement and recitals only.

THIS DECLARATION OF TRUST is made this   day of **6–012** 200
BY [X] and [Y] both of   [*address*] (hereinafter called "the Trustees" which expression shall where the context so admits include the trustee or trustees for the time being hereof)

WHEREAS:

(A) By a transfer dated   [*X*] (hereinafter called "the Settlor") transferred [*100*] Ordinary Shares of £1.00 each in [*XYZ*] Limited to the Trustees the said shareholding being designated "[*AX*]" Account

(B) The Trustees make this Declaration to confirm the terms upon which they have held and continue to hold such shareholding

NOW IT IS HEREBY DECLARED as follows:

1 In this deed where the context so admits
(A) "the Trust Fund" means:

   (i) the said [*100*] Ordinary Shares of £1.00 each in [*XYZ*] Limited designated "[*AX*]" Account
     etc

7

Indivisible assets

1. Introduction

7–001 It may be physically impossible to divide an asset, such as a painting, and yet the owner may wish to share ownership of it with another, either for commercial reasons or to reduce a potential liability to Inheritance Tax. Where there is an asset which is indivisible, it is appropriate that such an asset is the subject of a declaration of trust where ownership is to be shared. An inter vivos transfer of chattels can be made either by deed or by delivery. The benefit of a transfer of ownership by deed is evidential, a declaration of trust will give evidence of the date of the transfer.(It is not intended to deal here with the specialised area of shares in livestock (for instance a racehorse).

Similarly, an individual may be owed a sum of money and decide to transfer part of this to another, but not wish to upset his relationship with the debtor by outwardly bringing a third party into the transaction. A declaration of trust is again therefore a suitable medium to effect what is required.

2. Declaration of Trust of Chattels

7–002 If an owner of chattels wishes to give an interest therein to others, whilst this can be done through the medium of a declaration of trust, the parties should be aware of some potential problems.

(a) Inheritance tax

When making a declaration of trust of chattels the possibility of attack by the Revenue under the Reservation of Benefit rules (see Introduction p.7) should be considered. Where there is a gift, for example, of 50 per cent of the value of a chattel, one would maintain that this is a partial gift of an asset as opposed to a gift of an asset with a reservation (see *Commissioner for Stamp Duties of New South Wales v Perpetual Trustee Co* [1943] A.C. 425 and *Ingram v IRC* 2000 1 A.C. 293). However, if the possession or use of the chattels remains with the donor, even if the reservation of benefit rules do not apply there is likely to be a deemed benefit under the pre owned assets legislation from April 5, 2005 resulting in a charge to income tax. These charges can of course be avoided if the donor gives up possession and use of the chattels.

If the chattel concerned is already National Heritage Property (IHTA 1984, s.31) then provided the usual undertaking is given by the donee IHT considerations may not arise (IHTA 1984, ss 32(5), 32A(8)).

It should be noted that it is official practice not to treat an indemnity taken from the donee by the donor in respect of the liability to IHT imposed on the donors personal representatives by IHTA 1984, s.199(2) as a reservation of a benefit (see Dymond's Capital Taxes, para.5.441 (Sweet and Maxwell).

(b) Capital Gains Tax

A gift of chattels, or interest in them, is prima facie a chargeable **7–003** event for capital gains tax purposes (TCGA 1992).

Where an individual owns an asset already deemed to be of national interest and such asset is subject to an undertaking (as to viewing availability and so on) in favour of the Treasury, a gift of such asset (or part of it) will not incur liability to Capital Gains Tax provided the donee gives a similar undertaking (TCGA 1992, s.258(3)).

There is no capital gains tax payable if the consideration on the disposal of tangible moveable property amounts to £6,000 or less (TCGA 1992, s.262). Where the consideration exceeds £6000, the chargeable gain is limited to five thirds of the excess (s.262(2)). Where the disposal is of an interest in such tangible moveable property, this relief is adjusted (s.262(5)). There are of course specific rules relating to the disposal of a set of items (e.g. chairs) to prevent relief being claimed in respect of individual items forming a set (s.262(4)).

(c) Bills of Sale Act 1878 and Bills of Sale Act (1878) Amendment Act 1882

7–004 These Acts were designed, *inter alia*, to protect a money-lender advancing money on the security of chattels which appeared to belong to the possessor, when in fact they had already been sold to a third party or mortgaged to him. A declaration of trust by way of gift would not appear to fall within the provisions of the Acts (which would require registration as a bill of sale) (see *French v Gething* [1922 1 KB 236] and *Koppel v Koppel* [1966] 2 All E.R. 187), but if there is to be an element of sale (albeit at an under-value) and the chattels remain in the possession of the transferor, then it would appear that registration is necessary (see further Fisher and Lightwood's Law of Mortgage (11th ed., Butterworths, 2001)).

3. DECLARATION OF TRUST OF PART OF A DEBT

7–005 If a person owed money wishes to give that entitlement away, or sell it, he can assign the debt by a Deed of Assignment (see example in Kelly's Draftsman (18th edition at p.286, Butterworths)), notice to the debtor of such deed being usually given by the assignee so as to effect his title against third parties (Law of Property Act 1925, s.136). Gains on the disposal of a debt (other than a debt on security) by the original creditor are exempt from capital gains tax. Where part of a debt is to be assigned, a declaration of trust by the person entitled to receive payment is appropriate. Such a declaration is useful where for inheritance tax reasons, for example, it is desired to give away part of a sum of money owed. This gets the seven year period running without having to wait for the receipt of the cash.

It is submitted that this will be a partial gift and that the reservation of benefit rules do not apply (see above, p.137).

4. STEPS TO BE TAKEN

(a) Stamp Duty

7–006 Following Finance Act 2003, the declarations of trust do not attract stamp duty nor require any stamp duty certificate.

(b) Notice

If an interest in chattels is gifted, and these are not in the possession of the donor, notice should be given to the storage firm, gallery, museum, etc., that the chattels should now be held on behalf of the donor and the donees.

(c) Insurance

Similarly, insurance of the chattels the subject of the declaration of trust should be amended into the names of the donor and the donees. Payment of the premium should be shared appropriately to evidence the split in ownership.

Precedent 42—Gift of share in chattels (or proceeds of sale thereof).

7–007 THIS DECLARATION OF TRUST is made this   day of 200

BETWEEN:

(1)   ("the Donor") of   [*address*] and

(2)   ("Son")   of   [*address*]   and ("Daughter") of   [*address*]

WHEREAS:

(A) Following the death of [*Donor's Uncle*] on   200 the Donor became absolutely entitled to the picture details of which are given in the Schedule hereto ("the Picture") [*subject to an Undertaking to HM Treasury in respect thereof*]

(B) The Donor is proposing to sell the Picture and is in negotiation concerning such sale

[(C) On any sale of the Picture Inheritance Tax will become or will be deemed to be payable]

[(D) The picture is presently on loan at no charge to [*Gallery or Museum*] pending sale]

(E) The Donor is desirous of making an immediate gift of such percentage of the value of the Picture as represents one half of the proceeds of sale thereof after deduction therefrom of the costs of sale [*and any IHT liability*]

NOW THIS DEED WITNESSES as follows:

1 The Donor HEREBY DECLARES that henceforward he holds the Picture and the proceeds of sale thereof as Trustee UPON TRUST:

    (a) as to one half for himself

    (b) as to the other half for Son and Daughter in equal shares absolutely

SUBJECT to deducting from any proceeds of sale [*any IHT liability in respect thereof and*] any costs of sale of the same

2 Son and Daughter accept the gift hereby made in the shares aforesaid as their signatures hereto hereby testify

3 Son and Daughter respectively covenant to indemnify the Donor and his estate against any liability to Inheritance Tax arising by reason of the death of the Donor and in respect of the gift the subject of this deed

IN WITNESS whereof this Declaration has been duly executed the day and year before written

SCHEDULE

[*Description of Picture and its present whereabouts*]

SIGNED and delivered as a
DEED by the Donor in the
presence of:

SIGNED and delivered as a
DEED by Son in the presence
of:

SIGNED and delivered as a
DEED by Daughter in the
presence of:

Precedent 43—Gift of share of debt owed to donor.

7–008 THIS DECLARATION OF TRUST is made this   day of
                  200
       BETWEEN (1)   of   [address] ("the
       Donor") and (2)   of   [address] ("the
       Recipient")

       WHEREAS:

       (A) [name and address of Debtor] owes £   ("the
       Debt") to the Donor

       (B) The Donor is desirous of giving to the Recipient entitlement
       to [one half] of the Debt ("the Assigned Part") and has agreed to
       make this Declaration accordingly

       NOW THIS DEED WITNESSES as follows:

       1 The Donor declares himself a trustee of the Assigned Part being
       part of the Debt and all interest due or to become due upon the
       Assigned Part and the full benefit and advantage of the Assigned
       Part in trust for the Recipient absolutely

       2 The Recipient hereby covenants to indemnify the Donor and his
       estate against any liability to Inheritance Tax arising by reason of
       the death of the Donor in respect of the gift the subject of this
       Deed

          IN WITNESS whereof this Declaration has been duly executed
       the day and year before written

       SIGNED and delivered as a
       DEED by the Donor in the
       presence of:

       SIGNED and delivered as a
       DEED by the Recipient
       in the presence of:

8

In conjunction with wills—
the half secret trust
and mutual wills

1. Introduction

The concept of the secret or half secret trust always seemed to be **8–001**
the subject of a Law School lecture that would never have
relevance in modern practice. This is not the case.

As a reminder:
1 the fully secret trust is just that; the will contains what appears
to be an outright gift to X. To be effective as a trust, there will of
course have to be communication of the trust to X and acceptance
by him of the same; *Blackwell v Blackwell* [1929] A.C. 318 (see
further Williams on Wills (8th ed. Butterworths) pp. 394–400).
Otherwise the donee is entitled to take the gift for his own benefit
(Re Stead [1900] 1 Ch. 237). It is of course vital that the testator
can trust X. Such a gift covers for example a legacy for the benefit
of the mistress not known to the deceased's spouse; and
2 the half secret trust; the will contains a gift to X and Y as
trustees to be held upon trusts previously communicated to them
(i.e. it is clear on the face of the will that there is a trust and that
it has been accepted by the trustees).

2. The Reason for a Half Secret Trust

A will once proved becomes a document of public record. Whilst **8–002**
an *inter vivos* gift does not become public knowledge and is
therefore the best method of keeping a gift secret, the testator
may not be in a position to make such a gift during his lifetime.
On death, he may wish to benefit either individuals, charities or

other bodies of which his family may disapprove or which might surprise the public. Such benefits can be kept from the public gaze through the medium of the half secret trust. The will might for instance contain a gift as follows:

> "I give the sum of £10,000 to X and Y as trustees to distribute the same in accordance with the provisions of a Declaration of Trust executed by them immediately prior to the execution of this my Will".

or

> "My Trustees shall transfer my Residuary Estate (as herein-before defined) to X and Y as trustees to hold the same in accordance with the provisions of a Declaration of Trust executed by them immediately prior to the execution of this my Will".

Such declaration, not being a testamentary disposition, does not require to be produced for probate, so its contents remain a secret.

3. THE REQUIREMENTS OF A HALF SECRET TRUST

8–003   The beneficial trusts of the gift must be defined and communicated to the trustees on or before the execution of the will (Re Bateman's Will Trusts; *Brierley v Perry* [1970] 3 All E.R. 817) and accepted by the trustees (*Blackwell v Blackwell*, above).

The declaration cannot contain any provision for alteration or revision of the trusts (Re Jones [1942] Ch. 328). The testator must therefore be clear prior to making his will what the beneficial interests of the half secret trust are to be. In Re Pugh's Will Trust [1967] 3 All E.R. 337 a gift

> "to my trustee absolutely and I direct him to dispose of the same in accordance with any letter or memorandum which I may leave with this my Will and otherwise in such manner as he may in his absolute discretion think fit"

was declared as a trust void for uncertainty as there was no letter or memoranda—the property in that case passed to the persons entitled on intestacy.

4. Enforceability of a Half Secret Trust

It is essential that the testator should be able to trust the trustees **8–004** of the half secret trust. Unless he has communicated to the beneficiaries the fact that they are to benefit, then there is little to stop unscrupulous trustees acting in clear breach of trust and retaining the assets bequeathed to them for their own benefit. Reliable trustees and some communication to beneficiaries prior to death would appear to be sensible.

5. Inheritance Tax

On the face of it a legacy or gift of residue through the medium of **8–005** a half secret trust might not appear to qualify for any exemption for Inheritance Tax purposes.

However, if the underlying gift is for the benefit of an exempt person (the secret wife perhaps) or exempt institution (a registered charity or recognised political party for instance; see IHTA 1984, ss.23 and 24) then IHT relief should be available: this will of course require production of the half secret trust document to the Capital Taxes Office (see IHTA 1984, ss.17(b) and 143).

6. Mutual Wills

Mutual wills arise when two parties (usually a husband and wife) **8–006** agree to execute non- revocable wills in a certain form (usually mirror wills conferring reciprocal benefits). The agreement is enforced after the death of the first testator by means of a constructive trust which prevents the survivor disposing of the property so as to defeat their mutual intentions.

It can often be the case that the survivor does wish to dispose of the property elsewhere perhaps because he remarries, and difficulties can then ensue in establishing whether an agreement did in fact exist and if so what is the precise nature, scope and effect of the trust imposed on the estate of the survivor. For these reasons practitioners often dissuade clients from entering into mutual wills.

Where a couple want to ensure that property passes to their children on the death of the survivor it may be better to consider creating a life interest trust for the survivor with appropriate powers to apply capital.

Although the making of similar wills for example on the part of husband and wife should not of itself invoke the doctrine of mutual wills (see *Birch v Curtis* 2002 EWHC 1158), it may be sensible in those circumstances to include a declaration in the will to the effect that there is no agreement as to non revocation (see Precedent 45). If after proper consideration mutual wills are to be entered into, then again the position should be stated explicitly by adding a declaration to the revocation clause (see Precedent 46).

In order to comply with Law of Property (Miscellaneous Provisions) Act 1989, s.2 both parties to mutual wills should also sign a separate agreement where land is involved (Healey v Brown 2002 WTLR 849).

7. Steps to be Taken

(a) Stamp Duty

8–007 Following Finance Act 2003, a declaration of trust which does not relate to shares will not attract stamp duty.

(b) Safe-keeping of the declaration

If the trustees of the half secret trust are the executors of the will, then there is no objection to the declaration being lodged for safe-keeping with it. If the trustees are not the executors, then to keep the trust secret it should be kept separate from the will, and the executors left details of the whereabouts of the "secret trustees".

Precedent 44—Declaration of trust of property to be given on half secret trust under a will.

THIS DECLARATION OF TRUST is made this   day of **8–008**
200
BY X of   [address]   and Y
of   [address] ("the Trustees")

WHEREAS:

(A) JOHN SMITH of   [address] ("the Testator") by his Will ("the Will") to be executed immediately after this Declaration has left the sum of [£10,000] to the Trustees to distribute the same in accordance with the provisions hereof

(B) The Trustees make this Declaration to set out those provisions

NOW IT IS HEREBY DECLARED that if and when the Will becomes effective and the sum of [£10,000] is received by the Trustees they shall hold the same:

  (a) as to [£5,000] for A absolutely

  (b) as to [£5,000] for B (being the child of A) absolutely but with power to pay the same should B be a minor at the time of the Testator's death to the parent or guardian of B whose receipt shall be a good discharge.

IN WITNESS whereof this Declaration has been duly executed the day and year before written

SIGNED and DELIVERED as
a DEED by X in the
presence of:

SIGNED and DELIVERED as
a DEED by Y in
the presence of:

Precedent 45—Declaration in respect of reciprocal (but not mutual) will.

8–009 I [testator] of [address] revoke all former wills and codicils made by me and declare this to be my last will. Although my wife [name] has today executed a will in similar terms to this we have agreed that our wills shall not be mutual wills and that each of us is free to revoke or alter our respective wills before or after the death of the other.

Precedent 46—Declaration in respect of mutual will

I [testator] of [address] revoke all former wills and codicils made **8–010**
by me and declare this to be my last will. My wife [name] has
today executed a will in similar terms to this will and we have
agreed that neither of us shall revoke nor alter our respective wills
after the death of the survivor of us.

Index

Instruction for use of the companion disc

Introduction

These notes are provided for guidance only. They should be read and interpreted in the context of your own computer system and operational procedures. It is assumed that you have a basic knowledge of WINDOWS. However, if there is any problem please contact our help line on 020 7393 7266 who will be happy to help you.

CD Format and Contents

To run this CD you need at least:

IBM compatible PC
CD-ROM drive
Microsoft Word 6.0/95

The CD contains data files of the clauses in this book. It does not contain software or commentary.

Installation

The following instructions make the assumption that you will copy the data files to a single directory on your hard disk (e.g. C:\Declarations of Trust).

Open your **CD Rom drive**, select and double click on **setup.exe** and follow the instructions. The files will be unzipped to your **C drive** and you will be able to open them from the new **C:\Declarations of Trust** folder there.

LICENCE AGREEMENT

Definitions

l. The following terms will have the following meanings: "The PUBLISHERS" means Sweet & Maxwell of 100 Avenue Road, London NW3 3PF (which expression shall, where the context admits, include the PUBLISHERS' assigns or successors in business as the case may be) of the other part on behalf of Thomson Books Limited of Cheriton House, North Way, Andover SPI0 5BE.

"The LICENSEE" means the purchaser of the title containing the Licensed Material.

"Licensed Material" means the data included on the disk;

"Licence" means a single user licence;

"Computer" means an IBM-PC compatible computer.

Grant of Licence; Back up copies

2. (1) The PUBLISHERS hereby grant to the LICENSEE. a non-exclusive, non-transferable licence to use the Licensed Material in accordance with these terms and conditions.

(2) The LICENSEE may install the Licensed Material for use on one computer only at any one time.

(3) The LICENSEE may make one back-up copy of the Licensed Material only, to be kept in the LICENSEE's control and possession.

Proprietary Rights

3. (1) All rights not expressly granted herein are reserved.

(2) The Licensed Material is not sold to the LICENSEE who shall not acquire any right, title or interest in the Licensed Material or in the media upon which the Licensed Material is supplied.

(3) The LICENSEE shall not erase, remove, deface or cover any trademark, copyright notice, guarantee or other statement on any media containing the Licensed Material.

(4) The LICENSEE shall only use the Licensed Material in the normal course of its business and shall not use the Licensed Material for the purpose of operating a bureau or similar service or any online service whatsoever.

(5) Permission is hereby granted to LICENSEES who are members of the legal profession (which expression does not include individuals or organisations engaged in the supply of services to the legal profession) to reproduce, transmit and store small quantities of text for the purpose of enabling them to provide legal advice to or to draft documents or conduct proceedings on behalf of their clients.

(6) The LICENSEE shall not sublicense the Licensed Material to others and this Licence Agreement may not be transferred, sublicensed, assigned or otherwise disposed of in whole or in part.

(7) The LICENSEE shall inform the PUBLISHERS on becoming aware of any unauthorised use of the Licensed Material.

Warranties

4. (1) The PUBLISHERS warrant that they have obtained all necessary rights to grant this licence.

(2) Whilst reasonable care is taken to ensure the accuracy and completeness of the Licensed Material supplied, the PUBLISHERS make no representations or warranties, express or implied, that the Licensed Material is free from errors or omissions.

(3) The Licensed Material is supplied to the LICENSEE on an "as is" basis and has not been supplied to meet the LICENSEE'S individual requirements. It is the sole responsibility of the LICENSEE to satisfy itself prior to entering this Licence Agreement that the Licensed Material will meet the LICENSEE's requirements and be compatible with the LICENSEE's hardware/software configuration. No failure of any part of the Licensed Material to be suitable for the LICENSEE's requirements will give rise to any claim against the PUBLISHERS.

(4) In the event of any material inherent defects in the physical media on which the licensed material may be supplied. other than caused by accident abuse or misuse by the LICENSEE, the PUBLISHERS will replace the defective original media free of charge provided it is returned to the place of purchase within 90 days of the purchase date.

The PUBLISHERS' enure liability and the LICENSEE's exclusive remedy shall be the replacement of such detective media.

(5) Whilst all reasonable care has been taken to exclude computer viruses, no warranty is made that the Licensed Material is virus free. The LICENSEE shall be responsible to ensure that no virus is introduced to any computer or network and shall not hold the PUBLISHERS responsible.

(6) The warranties set out herein are exclusive of and in lieu of all other conditions and warranties, either express or implied, statutory or otherwise.

(7) All other conditions and warranties, either express or implied, statutory or otherwise, which relate in the condition and fitness for any purpose of the Licensed Material are hereby excluded and the PUBLISHERS shall not be liable in contract or in tort for any loss of any kind suffered by reason of any defect in the Licensed Material (whether or not caused by the negligence of the PUBLISHERS).

Limitation of Liability and Indemnity

5. (1) The LICENSEE shall accept sole responsibility for and the PUBLISHERS shall not be liable for the use of the Licensed Material by the LICENSEE, its agents and employees and the LICENSEE shall hold the PUBLISHERS harmless and fully indemnified against any claims, costs, damages, loss and liabilities arising out of any such use.

(2) The PUBLISHERS shall not be liable for any indirect or consequential loss suffered by the LICENSEE (including without limitation loss of profits, goodwill or data) in connection with the Licensed Material howsoever arising.

(3) The PUBLISHERS will have no liability whatsoever for any liability of the LICENSEE or any third party which might arise.

(4) The LICENSEE hereby agrees that

(a) the LICENSEE is best placed to foresee and evaluate any loss that might be suffered in connection with this Licence Agreement;

(b) that the cost of supply of the Licensed Material has been calculated on the basis of the limitations and exclusions contained herein; and

(c) the LICENSEE will effect such insurance as is suitable having regard to the LICENSEE's circumstances.

(5) The aggregate maximum liability of the PUBLISHERS in respect of any direct loss or any other loss (to the extent that such loss is not excluded by this Licence Agreement or otherwise) whether such a claim arises in contract or tort shall not exceed a sum equal to that paid as the price for the title containing the Licensed Material.

Termination

6. (1) In the event of any breach of this Agreement including any violation of any copyright in the Licensed Material, whether held by the PUBLISHERS or others in the Licensed Material, the Licence Agreement shall automatically terminate immediately, without notice and without prejudice to any claim which the PUBLISHERS may have either for moneys due and/ or damages and/or otherwise.

(2) Clauses 3 to 5 shall survive the termination for whatsoever reason of this Licence Agreement.

(3) In the event of termination of this Licence Agreement the LICENSEE will remove the Licensed Material.

Miscellaneous

7. (1) Any delay or forbearance by the PUBLISHERS in enforcing any provisions of this Licence Agicenient shall not be construed as a waiver of such provision or an agreement thereafter not to enforce the said provision.

(2) This Licence Agreement shall be governed by the laws of England and Wales, If any difference shall arise between the Parties touching the meaning of this Licence Agreement or the rights and liabilities of the parties thereto, the same shall be referred to arbitration in accordance with the provisions of the Arbitration Act 1996, or any amending or substituting statute for the time being in force.

Disclaimer

The precedents and commentary contained in this publication are not tailored to any particular factual situation. Precedents in this publication may be used as a guide for preparation of documentation, which may be provided to clients, but distribution to third parties is otherwise prohibited. Precedents are provided "as is" without warranty of any kind, express or implied, including but not limited to fitness for a particular purpose. The publishers and the author do not accept any responsibility for any loss of whatsoever kind including loss of revenue, business, anticipated savings or profits, loss of goodwill or data or for any indirect consequential loss whatsoever to any person using the precedents or acting or refraining from action as a result of the material in this publication.